I0069090

NATURE TO BUSINESS

Wisdom From My Garden

NATURE TO BUSINESS

Wisdom From My Garden

Kathleen Nakfoor, Ed.D., MBA, MSIS, BSN

Nature to Business: Wisdom from My Garden

Copyright © 2022 by Kate Nakfoor

All rights reserved. No part of this publication may be reproduced, distributed or transmitted in any form or by any means without prior written permission.

ISBN 978-1-952194-16-0

Cover art and design by Adam Barton

Book design by River Sanctuary Graphic Arts

Printed in the United States of America

Additional copies available from:

www.riversanctuarypublishing.com

amazon.com

River Sanctuary Publishing
P.O Box 1561
Felton, CA 95018
www.riversanctuarypublishing.com

Dedicated to the awakening of the New Earth

To Dad
who inspired this book

Acknowledgements

This book would not be possible without the editorial support of Magdalena Montagne. Magdalena has been at my side since the book was only an idea when she helped me lay out the first drafts five years ago. She has kept me accountable and supported me when I didn't think I could tolerate one more edit! I consider you a dear and lifelong friend. Thanks to the creative astuteness and sage insight of my son, Grant Buchwald, who conceptualized the cover and first suggested that my original book should be cleaved into two books (PlanKit®). I am grateful for Annie Elizabeth Porter and River Sanctuary Publishing for assistance through the publishing process. Special thanks to Annie Elizabeth for patience through the book's multiple iterations prior to printing. I so appreciate my daughter, Alex Buchwald's, help with the glossary and ongoing encouragement and support during the book's development. Thanks to Christy Goldspink who, as an experienced publisher and copy editor, urged me to write this book because of its unique concept. I'm indebted to the friends and family who have given me the fortitude to complete this book.

Author's Note:

As you read this book, keep in mind that my garden is a metaphor for your relationships and organizations. While the references to my garden are real, the analogy is meant to teach, to stimulate thought and inspire reflection on your personal and business life.

CONTENTS

Chapter 2 Analysis of Kate's Garden Using the PlanKit®

SUMMER

Chapter 3 Genesis of Emergency Specialists Corporation (ESC)

A life without nature is not living!

Introduction

My Garden Is My Sanctuary

Calm overwhelms me when surrounded by nature. No matter what daily stress I face, stepping into my garden lifts all tension, exhales away worry. Walking among the cypress, inhaling the scent of eucalyptus not only eases the strain of life's pressures but envelopes me with serenity. Even on the foggiest days, I'm wrapped in peacefulness.

While gardening, all my senses ignite as I touch and smell—and see the brush strokes of Mother Nature's artistry painted across the landscape; the wind and sun blanching my skin, engrossed in the interconnectedness of nature's pure elements. One must be present as Nature makes herself known—alive to us if we partake in what she offers.

I had been gardening for at least 15 years when my father passed away. My father and I had been very close and I was devastated. It was September 17, 2006, and I felt as if my heart had been severed and half-buried with my dad.

Prior to this time, I had an approximate half-acre of landscaped garden enclosed in a stucco-walled perimeter around my home, managed nicely with some help. But now I needed to redirect my sadness toward something positive. I decided to take a half-acre of my property that was unkempt—full of woody pepper trees and

1

cast aside lawn debris—and design a garden for my dad. I turned my pain into a goal that both honored my father and filled a void with a different love by creating a place of solace and natural beauty.

FROM NATURE TO BUSINESS

At the time of my father's death, gardening was not the only thing occupying my energy. I led NakIVHealth, delivering business consultancy to healthcare providers, namely physicians and hospitals. I taught graduate-level Organizational Theory, Leadership and Organizational Analysis for over a decade at the University of San Francisco. I had earned two master degrees and a doctorate degree, developed three businesses, including Emergency Specialist Corporation, I was a wife and mother of two and had been an Emergency Department nurse for 16 years prior to this time.

As I thrust into the design of my garden, from hardscape to clearing and prepping the land, *I uncovered the parallels between building a business and building a garden.* But it wasn't until the moments when I was completely immersed in gardening, without the distraction of unnatural noise, that the epiphanies emerged without provocation. *What became clear to me was that much of what we need to know about the interrelationships within a business can be learned from nature.* In the quiet solitude of my garden, I recognized that similarities between theories I had espoused as a consultant and educator seemed drawn from the natural world. For example, while extricating the dense layers of mint vines, the pervasiveness of weeds and my efforts to eradicate them reminded me of the competing forces in the workplace and the competition for resources and sustainability. Some days I felt as if I walked into a war zone when entering my garden and I was reminded of Kurt Lewin's theory of competing forces.[1] Lewin's Force Field Analysis (FFA)[2] explains the driving and restraining forces that move us toward and away from reaching our goals. Firsthand, I came to appreciate the significance of Porter's Model of Five Forces[3]—understanding the critical need to scan and assess one's competitive forces.

> *I discovered the parallels between building a business and building a garden. What became clear to me was that much of what we need to know about the interrelationships within a business can be learned from nature.*

Competition for resources in nature is no different than competing for resources and market share in business. Michael Porter's Model of Five Forces,[4] a tool I introduced to graduate students analyzing organizations, is pertinent when studying both established and emerging companies. The Model demonstrates the importance of scanning external forces for the power of buyers and suppliers, as the threat of substitution is ever present. This tool is useful at every stage of the business cycle.[5] Knowledge of one's garden and its environment is critical to success, just as in business.

As you read this book and see the similarities between nature and business presented in the following pages, you will be invited to reflect on your business and your life. I will be presenting a variety of tools you're encouraged to utilize both personally and professionally for analysis and reflection. I have used all these strategies in my consulting practice over the years, and taught these approaches to graduate students of Organizational Theory for over 17 years.

In addition to the tools I introduce for use in your business, each chapter includes opportunities for contemplation and writing.

In Part one, I ask you to reflect on our vast ecosystem with Mother Nature orchestrating her infinite pieces into an interconnected symphony that includes my garden. In Chapters one and three, I draw parallels between the life cycle of the rose and business cycle of a company—seed, growth, establishment, maturity and decline. In chapter one, I begin to weave together the interconnections between all that Mother Nature shares toward the understanding of the development, design and growth of an organization. Just as you need a design for your garden, you need a business design.

We all need a strategic plan, whether for our business, personal life or for our gardens. Chapter two is a retrospective analysis of what I did right and what I overlooked while creating the garden for my dad. To perform this analysis, I used a nine-step process that I developed and service-marked called PlanKit®, utilizing established business tools and concepts. PlanKit® is a step-wise methodology that begins with your vision for change, a desire to move from where you are to where you want to be, and, after completing a series of introspective questions, you will have created a strategy for realizing the change you envisioned. By methodically implementing these principles, organizations and individuals have successfully achieved their goals after long periods of inertia, identified gaps, improved efficiencies, maximized resources, accelerated their growth and development, and moved from where they were to where they wanted to be.

In chapter three, I share the narrative of starting my first business as a naïve, 28 year old with a vision for disrupting the field of nursing by independently contracting emergency department and critical care areas of hospitals. I impart the ups and downs of a young entrepreneur who forged ahead with a great vision for independent contracting and expertise in the field of emergency nursing, but without experience operating a business. It is my hope, for those of you considering starting a small business, that you will glean lessons from my experience.

Chapters five and six are dense with the "boring but important stuff." Chapter five gives you an overview of systems theory. Systems theory is a complex theory I have simplified in order for you to utilize—to view every encounter and problem from a new perspective—*we live in a world of infinite systems that are all interconnected. In order to solve a problem in one part of a system we need to understand the interrelationships between all the other parts of the system.*[6]

> *It is my hope that the wisdom gathered in my garden—from nature to business—will help you achieve your goals and your garden will be eternally healthy and thriving.*

Chapter six provides the reader with a short course in organizational theory, including leadership and group dynamics. Did you know your family, community, workplaces and even your garden is an organization? Throughout the book I weave together the common threads interlacing business organizations and Mother Nature's immense world, culminating in the thesis of this book—*that all living things are interconnected.*

My book concludes with a section on the Coronavirus (Covid-19). What better example of the interconnectedness of all living things than the personal and economic ravages of the Covid-19.

I have woven sage quotes and a few of my poems throughout the book for inspiration and reflection.

Recognizing the parallels between nature and business was purely an inspiration—I was/am a conduit for uncovering these similarities. I believe the grief that led me to create this dedicated place of nature for my dad, in turn, ultimately led to the writing of *From Nature to*

Business; Wisdom From My Garden. The raw heartache after losing my father—the genesis for my garden—provided me the natural space to uncover the analogies between nature and business.

> *We live in a world of infinite systems that are all interconnected. In order to solve a problem in one part of a system we need to understand the interrelationships between all the other parts of the system.*

My sadness has softened into daily memories of my dad. I now have a different kind of relationship with him. He still offers me love through the radiance of my garden, the luminosity of falling stars and even in the midst of the fog—dad is my co-author.

My garden is my most beautiful masterpiece.

Claude Monet[7]

Nature Speaks

Nature has spoken for
billions of years

the trees speak in letters
and declare to the Gods

each sapling a rune
with something to say

we're too fledgling to discern
too young to know how to pray

infantile humans
crawling on two legs

trying to comprehend
the tongue of the trees

when I ascend to the welkin
I, too, will know

PART I

My Garden

Ecosystem (macrosystem)

Every gardener knows about the impact of the conditions both near and distant within the vast ecosystem. Miriam Webster's definition of ecosystem is *the complex of a community of organisms functioning as an ecological unit.* Abiotic, non-living, systems such as the solar system are interdependent upon biotic, living, systems—from single-cell organisms to complex animals and plants. Natural disasters such as earthquakes, hurricanes, and fires will disrupt the ecosystem. Edward Lorenz reminds us that the flapping of butterfly wings can cause changes to the ecosystem thousands of miles away.[8] The causes and effects on the ecosystem are infinite and far-reaching. Weather patterns, such as El Nino, and its typical successor, La Nina, have demonstrated severe global conditions wreaking havoc on farming, land, animals, and subsequently impacting all elements of the ecosystem, leading to drought, fires and resultant economic impact.[9]

Our gardens, just as all of nature, comprise a micro-ecosystem. For those designing a garden, a time-tested rule is to include a diverse habitat of species to create different dwellings for a variety of creatures—from microbial cells working in and on the soil to an array of animals and birds.

Good soil is the beginning foundation, providing the building blocks for healthy plants, and, in turn, the plants create habitat, food, and reproductive sites for insects, birds and animals. Attracting birds helps control pests and aids in reforestation and in maintaining the health of watersheds.

> *I found pleasure in digging down to the core of a problem, and recognized the importance of quality input for quality output.*

While in my garden, it's extraordinary to see the interconnectedness of all the elements that share the ecosystem: sunlight extending its rays reaching playfully upon the ocean, as hawks soar overhead seizing the eastward wind currents; a turkey vulture perched atop the nearby telephone pole—dodging attacks by the distressed starlings; scampering rabbits take refuge under the rock rose bushes, while snails backpack up the branches of my hibiscus, making basecamp on leaves like a box of See's chocolates sampling the assortment of flavors—deer inhaling my roses....oh no!

My soul aches without time spent in the garden. I need to be close to my plants and the earth, if even only to pull weeds or survey the latest invasion of gophers. I have no doubt there is a transfer of energy that reaches deep and nourishes my core.

Plants, like people, have their innate propensities to shade or sunlight, the need for more or less water and wind, and, like us, have a genetic make-up to hardiness, a weakness to some diseases, varying heights and a multitude of inherent characteristics. Plants know when to close their cupped flowers as dusk gathers, and lie dormant in the cool, short days of winter. Spring signals regrowth.

Reflect in Your Garden

Effective leaders take time for reflection. How much time do you take for regular reflection to clear your mind and make way for fresh, innovative ideas?

Let go of the day-to-day distractions. Spend a half-hour in a garden, walking in the park or a place in nature and reflect on what's around you.

This is your spring and a time for renewal, to grow and change one thing that you have been inspired to do.

My Garden (microsystem)

The foundation and development of a garden is the orchestration of a multitude of eco-instruments provided by Mother Nature. For example, ladybugs feed on pollen and will be enticed into your garden by plants such as coreopsis, dill, fennel, scented geraniums, and more; aphids are destructive to roses and the introduction of ladybugs can consume 50-60 aphids per day.[10] Bees also depend on pollen to feed their hives, and we depend on bees to embellish our gardens with flowers and food.

> *My soul aches without time spent in the garden. I need to be close to my plants and the earth, if even only to pull weeds or survey the latest invasion of gophers. I have no doubt there is a transfer of energy that reaches deep and nourishes my core.*

Despite having created an enviable garden before my father's death, executing this new piece of paradise would open my eyes to the difference between the daily tasks of gardening and *the art and science of gardening*. Prior to this time, I'd find an appealing plant and stick it in the ground. I had such a limited understanding of the multiple variables involved in creating a sustainable, ideal garden suited to my location's climate and soil. What I did know was that I could learn.

I undertook a newfound study of horticulture. I poured over rose catalogs, ordered every book on West Coast gardening, perused nurseries, and joined every rose society from San Francisco to Monterey. I loved scoring pots and plants at the flea market, resisting my old habit of grabbing any plant that caught my eye.

In my early days of gardening, I didn't know the basics, including distinguishing between an annual and a perennial. I related to the many friends who jump-start their gardens with plants received on Mother's Day but quickly abandon the idea for just about anything else. Many people, like my mom, God bless her, could only manage the yard with the workforce of my brothers. When we moved into our second home, flowering plants abounded. By year two, most of the luscious peonies were whacked off by the lawnmower blades, never to return. My sister yearningly admires the beautifully maintained but expensive gardens in her neighborhood and surrounding the mall. However, she prefers to bring home a one-quart plant purchased at the local supermarket and transplant it, plastic pot and all, into the larger clay pot—without adding soil! Rain is the only comfort that plant will ever receive. Just as I cook to survive, others dine daily on the finest cuisine. I would rather spend an hour pruning a mini rose, while others want a "mow once-a-week" kind of yard requiring minimal effort. Although it's important to be true to yourself and follow your passions, establishing a garden is best left in the hands of owners who are passionate about gardening. Those gardeners who wander the flea markets for pots, make a study of their garden, share soil combinations with other enthusiasts, own a library of garden books, and cannot wait for the next flower catalogs to arrive.

Anyone reading this who shares my passion for gardening understands the rising pulse and palpations as you enter a wholesale nursery *open to the public.* As the cost mounted, I'd tell myself *it's a good addiction.*

In the garden dedicated to my father, the task of creating a memorial sanctuary was daunting. I trudged through the dense, knee-high weeds, flicking back insect-infested brambles while avoiding hundreds of holes—ingress and egress to an underground squirrel complex. Drawing upon my business experience, I knew my vision had to be laid out in a strategic plan identifying clearly defined goals toward the finished product.

First, I designed and built a hardscape structure—realizing my vision of three segregated stucco semicircles to house the rose, vegetable and English gardens, each with specific water and soil needs. Next, I installed the underground irrigation system with multiple zones to accommodate the vast, half-acre area. I did not have a well-planned watering system; an oversight which would haunt me for years to come. I had two hundred yards of soil delivered, compacted for the lawn and to fill the three, approximately 40 square-foot spaces. Each circle was double-lined with aviary wire to mitigate the intrusion of gophers before any of the compost-enriched soil was added.

Soil type, moisture, sunlight, and wind exposure are prime factors influencing plant selection.[11] Plants grow best in communities and should be suited to your microclimate. Knowing the elements of your garden area will make you not only an important steward, but a part of the ecosystem you are encouraging and maintaining.[12]

I really had no business putting a rose garden in the foggy Central Coast of California, however, it was an essential part of what I loved and visualized. I looked forward to learning and meeting the challenge of sustaining such a complex puzzle. The rose garden would be hand watered, augmented with a drip irrigation watering system. For the English garden, I brought in plants suitable for ocean air, afternoon winds, and the limited variation in year-round climate. Three miles inland was an industry built around fruit trees, but due to the marine layer and limited cool ground in the winter, trees would not yield produce on land so close to the Pacific.

I grew complementary plants instead of my previous method of covering every inch of soil with the latest attractive blooming annual. I learned to plant from seed and a mix of bulbs, tubers and natives, sowing them at the appropriate time of year, and avoided plants that reseeded and consumed every spare inch of soil. I became a student of natural herbicides and pesticides, and learned to meet the multiple proclivities associated with each plant type; I found pleasure in digging down to the core of a problem, and recognized the importance of quality input for quality output.

Reflect in Your Garden

Augmenting the soil in the garden enriches its health. How are you augmenting the foundation of your company to improve the quality of your staff and products?

What are you doing to enrich your personal life?

*Describe what you do to strengthen personal relationships.
Do you go for a walk, garden, sit in the park, hike, or climb?
Describe your relationship with nature.*

Find one parallel between the miracles in nature and the miracles in your life and/or your business.

What are you doing to augment and enrich your business?

How do you stay informed and knowledgeable to remain a good steward of your personal and business community?

SPRING

Spring signals rebirth, a new beginning. The burst of spring blooms awake our senses to the fresh scents of narcissus, hyacinths, freesia and lilacs. Spring is just beginning in parts of our world while autumn descends upon the opposite hemisphere—a reminder of the ever-changing gardens throughout our grand ecosystem. As you ready your garden, just as you lay the foundation to your business, there are questions to be answered.

Let's begin our journey along a path in nature, or as we tend our gardens, to observe all that Mother Nature has to teach us about operating a business, as she operates her vast holdings on earth.

Mist

In the early hours of day
you scatter drops of Earth's nectar
awaken flower buds
from somnolence

the yawn of petals open
to welcome day's
first crest of light

husks of sepals unfold
awash in vapor
releasing a tepid aroma—
moist in green

fog's spray blankets
as ribbons of
flowers dance to
day's arousal

CHAPTER 1

The Life Cycle of a Rose

Y ou have an idea for a business, a seed, and before it can germinate it needs a thorough plan, solid design, the right leadership and individuals with the essential knowledge and skills to successfully execute the owners' vision while mitigating risks. A plant dies or a business fails due to a poor plan, or no plan. A business may originate from a great idea, a good seed, and perhaps a knowledge of everything there is to know about the seed, but lack information on all the essential elements to grow the seed and get the product to market. Great ideas with poor execution result in failure.

Mother Nature's innate sense of survival has taught us the importance of a design and a successful outcome.

GARDEN DEVELOPMENT AND DESIGN

Designing a garden reminds me of expectant parents creating that special surrounding to provide a safe and secure home for their soon-to-be son or daughter. I find it interesting that individuals starting a business don't realize it, too, needs a design. I'm not talking about architecture but how staff will communicate with vendors, customers, and each other (see Chapter 6).

A good starting point in garden design is to consider the topography of your landscape. Will your garden be on a hillside and need retaining walls, and how will you maximize your given space? Also, at the outset, ask yourself, "Who is this garden for?" Will the garden be for you and your adult friends only, or do you have children or pets, such as dogs and cats, or even farm animals? Do you want a formal garden or one that incorporates more wild elements?

Several factors must be considered when designing a garden: orientation to the sun, surrounding plants and vegetation, type of plants desired, how to best mitigate risks to your plants, type of soil, timing and location. What is the best orientation for your garden to capture the least damaging wind but the effervescence of the sun, and seize the splendor of all that Mother Nature offers?

Just as you might design a room in your house, you can plan themes to unify your garden spaces. For a large area you can create smaller themes that tie together, also in keeping with the hundreds of plants to choose from— about 6,500 species in California alone—you can certainly find the plants that will work for you.[13] Delighting in the present means you might want some immediate gratification of color using annuals and potted plants. As you plan for the future, consider plants' growth rate, maintenance needs and size at maturity.

Review the history of the land you now occupy and consider if the site or soil has been modified. I had excessive lime dumped at the site where my fireplace was constructed, and 30 years later nothing will grow in this area. Are you looking for plants with exceptionally intense fragrance? With water a scarce resource, many people are turning to native plants or at least resource-efficient ones.

What is the climate and microclimate where you reside? I live close to the ocean so the fog, wind, and small variations in temperature are considerations when selecting plants. I can begin my garden in March due to the milder California climate, whereas Midwesterners and East Coast residents will wait a bit longer. Is it your intent to have a low-maintenance garden including native or succulent plants, or one a bit more challenging—including roses or orchids? Depending on whether the soil is predominantly sand, clay, silt or gravel, you can determine what plants will thrive. Will your garden be filled with tasty herbs and veggies, or is your proclivity toward flowers? In business, as in creating a garden, do your due diligence to ensure your location is a match for the goals you seek.

Just as in business, the design of your garden is dynamic. In business, as in your garden, you must constantly scan the external environment to be ever vigilant to competition and predators. While in your garden, you'll observe damage from wind or pests—signaling that it's time for an adjustment. Soil tests should indicate the acidity or alkalinity (pH) of the soil and what amendments may be necessary to change its pH to meet the plants' needs.

Just as in business, you should benchmark the results of your garden against a variety of indicators, always being sure to compare the same variables to similar garden types. For example, you would not compare the time of year to plant summer bulbs in California to the timing for cold regions of the Midwest and East coast. Look at what grows best in your neighborhood, talk to locals and get to know the nearby nursery staff. Observe visual indicators such as wilting, buds that fail to open, or leaves that look like Swiss cheese, all indicators that intervention is needed. Consult the USDA hardiness zone map to determine the most suitable plants for your area.[14] Likewise, business owners need to constantly survey their customers, ask for feedback and, most importantly, listen to what the customers have to say—building a sincere, quality-driven relationship with their target market.

Timing is critical for the most favorable yield in the garden. Mother Nature provides the glorious change of seasons and the inherent communication she has with all her harvest, and informs the way we as gardeners do our work. Timing affects a great number of outcomes in business, as well. Harvesting Christmas trees in January is a loser; selling bathing suits in Fort Lauderdale during spring break is a winner. Planning a large crop of pumpkins to sell at the local farmers' market in December, or opening a steak-lovers restaurant next to a cow ranch (whew, what is that smell?) are poor ideas. I think you get the picture of what happens when you pique all the wrong senses. On the other hand, being first to market most often predicts a competitive advantage.[15]

Light of the Mischievous

Day, taking its afternoon slumber before dusk
the sun resting midway in the sky
blanketing the ocean with heat
I, too, lying immersed in splendid warmth

Arising to bask in the fleeting, cool breeze—
I'm spellbound by the frolicking
in the distant trees below

Mischievous angels foregoing their naps
for a few playful hours before nightfall
flickering about the trees
pricking water drops as they splashed

Lighting up the pine and eucalyptus, I could see them—
glimmering between the branches
like hundreds of lit sparklers and
falling tips of fireworks
frosting the ocean with glitter

The sun awakes, only to descend
spreading its curtain of light on
the other side of the horizon

the moon glides into view
caressing the dancing angels
asleep in his arms

THE SEED

In order to begin thinking about how closely the world of nature parallels the world of business, let's begin with one example, the rose, and its life cycle. In the ongoing pages you will be introduced (or reintroduced) to some theories that may guide you or stimulate your thinking when setting up a business or reinvigorating an existing one. Some parts of the cycle for your particular business may not follow exactly our humble rose plant—as is the case in nature, there are external forces at play as well as cycles within cycles. If you're not the scientific type, just relax and imagine a gorgeous rose—perhaps an old-fashioned variety: Gertrude Jekyll or Cecile Brunner, or hybrid teas, Mr. Lincoln, Peace, Just Joey and Double Delight, the kind whose aroma opens the heart and mind.

It takes approximately three years for a rose seed to germinate into a plant: Cut a rose hip in half to find the seed, and, after much preparation and natural elimination of viable seeds, one of many will root. Whether the root matures into a rose plant is dependent on a multitude of variables as it strengthens and overcomes natural barriers to survival. For those willing to take the additional risk, the cost is far less and enjoyment far greater to grow from seed. Few individuals actually want to grow roses from seed, as they want the immediate gratification of seeing the rose bud then bloom.[16] Do you want to delay the gratification of income for a number of years in college, as physician specialists do? You may choose to develop a trade to have more immediate income and the potential of being self-employed, or build another type of business over time. Creating a business is like growing a rose from seed, it's exciting to see your idea grow to fruition with patience over the long-term. In land development, the monetary profit of turning a large parcel of land into a subdivision produces a significantly higher rate of return than buying the developed lot, however, this poses a great deal more risk due to carrying costs, time and uncertainty. Tenacious insurance and

Each rose is a glorious gift—just as you are—set out to grace the earth in a special way.

real estate salespeople earn a more secure living with perseverance over time, building a referral business. Dollar cost averaging into a well-strategized portfolio of securities is recommended for a greater return over time versus a short-term, get-rich-quick course of action. Individuals who choose the long-term commitment of growing a business find the risks are higher but typically the rewards are greater.

It is important to dedicate adequate resources at the design and seed phase to avoid needing far more resources later on to mitigate risk, and to maintain a disease-free, well-tended garden. An essential resource necessary for a successful rose plant and garden is its soil. Many informative books exist on building rich soil which is really the foundation for any plant. Location in the garden, type and distance of nearby plants, and access to nutrients and water are also important considerations. We can plant superior rose seeds or plants, but without the energy and commitment of the gardener, even exceptional plants will fail. It is not enough to have water, sun, and soil, but instead some measure of how much water, sun, and blend of nutrients in the soil—all the key inputs to transform the seed/plant to the highest quality output.

In my coastal location, weaknesses may be the salt air, limited sun due to fog, and subsequent propensity of disease due to excess moisture. Pests such as spider mites and cutworms are tiny predators to roses. Other threats are deer, gophers, moles and rodents. Internal weaknesses must be augmented or complemented by strengths from other sources, internally or externally. For example, during the years of drought in California, vigilant watering was required. However, some plants will adapt to extreme conditions by deepening their roots. To compensate for the marine fog, first, I chose roses classified "hardy," more disease resistant and hybridized to withstand less favorable climates.[17] Next, I planted my roses in an area that received all-day sun. With a rolling canopy of fog I hand-watered the roses at their roots to spare them the added moisture from above. The sandy soil was glorious drainage, but a compost and mulch added density to retain water.

When creating a strong foundation, whether in a relationship, business or garden, solid underpinnings to support its future growth are essential. I was building a garden and fervent about prepping the soil to introduce new plants into an area colonized by an altogether different species in existence for many years. I even torched small areas to eradicate certain weeds—but the longevity of these plants is extensive. What obstacles will you need to overcome as you undertake your new business? In business, a relationship or garden, the convergence of multiple forces will result in something new.

Regardless of the energy I expended to introduce dahlias and vegetables into a decades-old weed-inhabited soil, the pervasive weeds would not relegate their first position to the newly-introduced dahlia bulbs and vegetable seeds. Some species simply will not survive without generations passing or variables being held constant, so that in time, the plant will either adapt to its surroundings or die.

Rather than eradicate from below, pulling plants out and decimating them, I had to control the external forces through watering and vigilant weeding. Despite my valiant efforts to assimilate plants I loved, such as gardenias, fruit trees, plumeria, peonies and lilacs, these plants would not grow successfully in my Pacific Ocean microclimate. Considering an infinite number of variations needed for change to occur, my energy was the crucial force in accounting for adaptation. Likewise, when starting one's own business, I learned firsthand, the willingness to expend an infinite amount of energy will be one of the most important resource for success and sustainability.

Dahlia

Your symmetry, the plot of the Gods.
My cupped hands admire your face
stroke its painted beauty
as you sing to life.

Delighting in the luminescence of your aura
sun's heat lures the corolla to unwrap
as nature's expression unfurls
from its moist, lime-green purse.

As days pass
you unfold to smile,
broader and broader
until your erect body
commands the gaze of all who pass.

Your grassy pouch evolves into
a dense circle of salmon-colored leaflets
growing longer as the leggy petals
lengthen into a plate-sized circle.

Displayed among a sorority of greens
corals unite in a dress of floral beauty
leaving all who see you in awe.

What pleasure
your short life gives
to all who hold you—
touch you
invite you to their table.

Reflect in Your Garden

How much time are you willing to spend building your business?

How do you maintain a balance between personal and business responsibilities?

As you navigate your day, how do you gauge whether you are remaining in balance— creating boundaries to keep a separation between your business and personal life?

As you plot the course of your new business venture, take a thorough inventory of risks and a plan to mitigate these risks.

How are you preparing to traverse the daily minefields you'll need to negotiate operating a business?

What are you doing, or planning to do, to keep reinventing your business and cultivate new customers?

GROWTH PHASE

Yearning and inquisitive, I step into my garden. Exhaling slowly, I once again witness the eruption of tender seedlings punctuating the earth. Spring has removed winter's blanket, exposing a spectrum of vivid pinks, purples, yellows and whites—an Easter-egg color palate. Inhaling the floating fragrances of hyacinths, daffodils and freesia, I am renewed. Blooms announce their splendor and signal a year of new growth.

However, I quickly come back to reality, realizing I should not get lost in the allure of the crocus and rich reds of ranunculi, because without my diligent oversight the growth of weeds and potential disease are all too imminent. While I have been indoors tending my starter seedlings, Mother Nature has laid down weed seeds during her "dormant" winter; meanwhile quiescent wind, water, scuttling pests and birds scatter her kernels. Under the ground, the juicy, virginal, fragrance of roots beckons all sorts of creatures to the springtime buffet.

With all its splendor this growth phase is one of the most rewarding times in the garden, bringing generous gifts; but it can also bring you to your knees. After weeks and months of preparation and work, you will be devastated if unprepared for the eruption of weeds or the invasion of pests. During this time, the importance of being an ever-vigilant steward—watering, weeding, tending to mitigate the emergence of unwanted pests and fungus—is essential. Reassess. You may need additional resources to avoid the destruction of the yield you worked so hard to produce: mulch to combat weeds, wrap new gopher baskets under and around plants and/or add soil amendments to keep the ground fertile and healthy.

It took ten years to build my rose garden. First, the Ralph Moore miniatures populated the 400 square foot stucco-enclosed circle.

After introducing nearly every rose into my garden that Ralph Moore hybridized, I began to envision a few of David Austin's old English roses at home in my garden. Over time, I amassed a collection of 70 David Austin roses intermixed with the dozen remaining miniatures. Only a rose grower understands the daily battles to control the gophers, moles, weeds, insects and fungus, let alone the innumerable hours expended to nurture and cultivate dozens of roses. Ah, but the scents, colors, the magic of creation. It is a passion.

A successful business takes passion and innumerable hours to cultivate return customers, reimagining products, adapting to constant change, making payroll, tracking regulatory compliance and ensuring cash flow. The trade-offs are many and the pay-offs are greater.

Be prepared for tomorrow.

After all those dedicated years of work I awoke one morning to a ravaged rose garden after a weekend of revelry by a family of deer.

Desecration of the Roses

Walking through the garden I once knew, I grieve the loss of my sanctuary of roses; roses I watered with love, pruned, nourished, topping off the old and admiring the new. Daily visits brought us close. I knew each of you by name; after all, I planted you, nurtured you, watched as your stock grew and branches budded then filled with blossoms. Mesmerized at the miracle of colors, the symmetry of your unfolding—ah, what perfection! Caressing your soft tufts of petals; I'd pick off the spotted and rusty leaves, comb the ground to keep neat your dress, and the floor around you—protecting your world from trouble. How I relish what was our garden together, but even I could not shield you from all harm.

Today I lament; only sadness fills me as I search the rubble of weeds and the decimated brims of the bushes, a sign the deer have filled their bellies with the yield I worked to enjoy. Oh, the collection of David Austin roses I selected over years. My favorites: Pat Austin, Rose Austin, Gertrude Jekyll, Pilgrim and Munstead Rose, were such an extravagance. And the hybrid teas I chose: Just Joey, Double Delight and the reddest of red, Mr. Lincoln. All whom I'd arrange in glass jars to share among friends; after all I'm just the steward for God's artwork.

You've occupied a place I once called a safe haven. Hoof tracks and your insatiable appetite— you care less as my treasures succumb, suffocating from the burden of your occupation. What gives you the right to invade then leave me without the option to fight back? You've taken over what I struggled hard to build for years.

I turned away from the decimated roses for years and more unwanted tenants moved in. Ah, yes, I pull the burrowed thistle, the tangled and spindly weeds buried deep and sucking the underground of the nourishment meant for my pinks, reds, crimson and yellows. Still these unwanted plants rise up then leave tomorrow's spores, the nuclei of next year's even greater yield. Your roots a tunnel, an under-the-earth-labyrinth. I don't even want the dirt of your roots—contaminated with seeds of your invasion.

While I am saddened by the destruction of my four-legged neighbors—it's instinctive. However, there is no accounting for man's insatiable appetite for land through annihilation and occupation.

History and Mother Nature have shown us that the quest for land is ever powerful and never ending. The poem below was inspired as I absorbed the essence of an evening outside safely at home. However, I was reminded that many across the world may be experiencing a far different experience.

Lydda to La Selva

I

a cacophony of crickets
snails backpack up deep blue delphiniums
earwigs snuggle under pots
and burrow in the crevice of every can
brigades of ants on assigned missions
fog's mist envelopes the green

the hoot of the owl breaks night's quiet
rabbits flee, gophers retreat
cats find refuge beneath the bush
stealth coyotes and hawks rival for earth's catch—
nature planned for such execution

percussive palm fronds
harmonize with the ocean
gazanias close for the night
leaves crinkle as rolly-polys drive steadfast to shelter
the full moon lit pathway

II

the full moon illuminates the carnage
a scattering of bullets awakens the sleeping villagers
thrusts of soldiers' boots splayed door after door
forcing families from their homes

into the streets
herded into mosques
extinguished—
a village vanquished

stillness signals the absence of life
tables set for tomorrow
bloodied buildings, ruby red roads
attempts to wash away
the suffocating stench of decay

bulldozed bodies crunch beneath the U.N. workers' feet
nightfall means kidnappings
fathers forever separated
snipers seeking random prey

III

humans venerate one moon and the circumference of stars
for some, dusk portends solace
for others nightfall foreshadows anguish
God asks the weeds and flowers to share the same land

As the growth phase continues into early summer, May and June's bursts of elegant, vivid roses glorify your garden, cast its spell, emitting piquant perfumes opening its blooms to venerate you. Time spent with these luscious blooms will be enjoyed far more if you strategically manage all the elements of your sanctuary of flora. Don't grow complacent gazing at the vivid, shiny, green-leafed roses—the aphids and fungus are lurking nearby.

MITIGATING RISKS

The growth phase of your garden, as well as your business, is an important time to strengthen your end product by providing all the right resources at the right times. Now it is essential to keep a watchful eye out to prevent and mitigate potential enemies and threats.

Making mistakes can be a great way to learn, however, planning and maintaining a garden, just as planning and maintaining a business, requires not only consideration of what may cause destruction/demise, but taking every precaution to avoid and prepare for such threats. First, identify the risks to your garden: weeds, suckers under rose root balls, gophers, insects and plant and soil diseases.

The Weed

Merriam-Webster Dictionary defines a weed as: *an unwanted plant, usually of vigorous growth, choking out more desirable plants, and in competition with pleasing plants.* I long ago conjured the idea that weeds are a metaphor for evil. There is never just one weed! This malicious plant always travels in numbers and is scattered by wind, birds, underground rodents and uninformed gardeners tilling their soil. Tremendous energy is expended to control this unwanted green; rodents don't seem interested, and, too often, despite the efforts to eradicate, the weeds take over. Many weeds have deep, vine-like roots making eradication costly and time-consuming. The pervasiveness of some weeds makes them impossible to destroy.

I tilled and torched these ubiquitous and tenacious plants, only to have them return again for many years. Withholding water and vigilant weeding was the only means to control, but not eradicate, such unwanted greenery.

Knowledge is the best prevention! For example, I should have known that tilling a pervasive weed such as wood sorrel (*Oxalis*), with its deep-rooted string of tiny bulbs, would only cause them to multiply exponentially. Consider each sprig of sweet clover (*Melitotus officinalis*) and its pouch of buried seeds. I was sure if I extricated the entire bag, collecting them in a never-again-to-be-seen dumpsite, I'd beat them. However, this was the worst thing I could have done, as I simply scattered the underground seedlings! You must identify and eliminate from the root! Do you search for the root cause of a problem or simply apply a quick fix?

Weeds are seasonal, just as theft and scams rise during Christmas time. One prevents such menaces by being proactive and hyper-vigilant; being armed with knowledge and applying it at the most efficacious time is the best means of preventing such hazards. In spring, we may use a pre-emergent or other natural herbicide to squelch the growth of weeds; in autumn we prepare for winter and new growth with matting and mulch after clearing the weeds. During the active growth period of summer, we keep the area around plants clean, applying natural oils and soaps as armor against pests and disease.

I equate weeds with individuals who take more than they contribute—using valuable resources such as healthcare, fire and safety, education and any number of public services, without contributing to the taxes that pay for such costs. Long-term utilization of resources without contributing to the growth of the economy, or giving back, is a cost we all share.

Some days, facing a weed-ridden garden I would ask myself, *"Is what I'm doing here better than doing something else? Is something I'm doing without compensation worth more than working for a monetary purpose?"* In business we call this ever-present question "opportunity cost." Opportunity cost is the tradeoff of time, money or anything of worth, in exchange for something else, ideally for greater worth or value. We make choices of how we "spend" our time, sometimes without realizing it.

> *What makes us believe that any plant or species can survive despite our desire to make it so?*

My anxiety level was directly related to the density of weeds. I could only overcome my angst by parsing the work into small areas until I saw progress, uncovering the beauty of my roses, dahlias and other flowering plants. I'm aware of the ongoing questions of *why would you work this hard and fight these relentless battles?* I believe any pleasure we derive will take work. What goals are you willing to work hard to achieve?

Managing Cash Flow

Managing cash flow—ensuring more cash coming in than going out—is critical to the solvency of a business. In business, an example of a cost that negatively correlates to producing income is a frivolous lawsuit and the onerous and never-ending rules and regulations imposed by the government that challenge a company's survival. In my lifetime I've seen physicians forced to evolve from solo practice to multi-specialty organizations due to the cost of compliance with burdensome regulations and to streamline costs. Many of the multi-specialty physician groups have been forced to sell to an oligopoly of hospitals merely to survive. Businesses are consolidating in order to manage costs and to give the *strength in numbers* idiom new meaning.

While attending a large medical conference, an attendee rose and posed the question, "*Why do we always have to talk about money when we talk about healthcare?*" According to the centers for Medicare and MediCal Services, national healthcare expenditures for 2018 were $3.6 trillion dollars and 17.9 percent of the gross domestic product (GDP).[18] In 2020 the national healthcare expenditure grew 9.7% to $4.1 trillion dollars and reached the 20 percent of GDP seven years earlier than predicted when U.S. healthcare spending is estimated to be $6 trillion dollars, 20 percent of our GDP, by 2027.[19]

Opportunity cost is the trade-off of time, money or anything of worth, in exchange for something else, ideally for greater worth or value. We make choices of how we "spend" our time, sometimes without realizing it.

Reflect in Your Garden

What do you do to continue learning and building more knowledge about yourself and/or business?

What did you forget to anticipate? Are you prepared for a glorious yield? In what ways did you not rehearse for the unpredictable?

Do you need to hire more staff for seasonal help? Did you budget for downturns in sales?

What goals are you willing to work hard to achieve?

Without Cash Flow There is No Business

In 2010, Panera Cares CEO Ron Shaich opened its first "pay what you can afford" restaurant in St. Louis. Panera Cares is a nonprofit arm of the Panera Restaurant chain. More Panera Cares Restaurants with the same model opened in Dearborn, Chicago, Portland and Boston. However, as of 2019, only one restaurant remains in Boston. The model was based upon paying customers compensating for those who did not, or paid less; a laudable concept but monetarily a loss. According to pundits, the CEO failed to understand the real world when non-paying customers were advised that this would be their only opportunity to accept such philanthropy this month. One elderly woman felt embarrassed upon leaving when she was advised that should she come more than once-a-month she would be required to pay. Of course, conditions and limitations had to be applied to such philanthropy.[20]

> **Neither nature nor businesses survive without managing its resources.**

My garden requires resources to thrive. One of the greatest risks to a new business is cash flow. A business must create a five-year estimate of income and expenses, including breakeven point.

Suckers

Roses not grown by seed or on their own root stock are created by the fusion onto another rose's root stock—the union of the two is what we call the bud union. Suckers grow at the point where the root stock and rose plant are fused. Suckers are shoots that grow directly from the root stock below the bud union, and need to be removed because such shoots will take over the original rose bush if left unattended. Novice rose growers may be allured by a sucker, as it grows voraciously with more roses and thorns than the healthy virginal plant. However, suckers utilize resources needed for the health of the rose bush, and every rose grower must be attentive to remove such interlopers ready for a take-over.

> *Suckers can be equated to the informal organization within a business, and can take over a company if unrecognized.*

Suckers can be equated to the informal organization within a business (see Chapter 6). The informal organization in business is the powerful network that is not included on the formal organizational chart. Without proper management, this network of influential and powerful individuals will gradually overtake the formal organization. Vigilant oversight is necessary to prevent such a coup. Or, better yet, run a business in such a manner so that your human resources are rewarded for productivity and group norms eliminate social loafing. We have all worked with social loafers who let other teammates do their work because it has to get done. Don't fall prey to the allure of manipulating human resources, vendors or customers who abuse resources at your expense. Even ants can destroy a tree.

Gophers and Insects

This section should be called *the war zone!* Yes, many days entering my garden, despite its solitude, brought anxiety and frustration over the incessant invasion of unwanted pests in the form of insects and vermin! While we need to share the land, there must be parameters and structure to grow crops and carve a place for a garden, as long as it respects the ecosystem: to be a good steward. I believe in sharing the land with that which is natural.

The double aviary wire deterred the gophers for one year; then came the day I found my 80 rose plants upheaved from below. Individual wire baskets resolved the problem quickly before the shock killed them. Moles left a trail of cracked earth along the shortest distance to the nearest meal.

I tried a multitude of deterrents: smelly socks, spearmint gum, certain plants, submerged noise makers, dried fox urine and more. So many sure-fired ideas were such failures—I could hear the gophers laughing at me. I will admit my cat soldiers do keep them on the run.

Rose pests are visible by the chewed leaves of cutworms, white specks of aphids sprinkled like a dose of heavy salt scattered over the rosebuds and the rust blanketed on the reverse of the leaf. To ignore the potential invaders is simply negligent. Methods exist to both mitigate and eradicate these vermin. Before doing anything that may cause long-term, deleterious results, like spraying pesticides, look for beneficial insects or other natural deterrents. For the organic gardener who controls pests without the use of biochemicals, products as accessible and inexpensive as baking soda, liquid soap, and vegetable oil can do wonders.

Living in harmony with the environment or macrosystem is essential to the survival of my roses, as well as the survival of our species.

Disease

An assortment of natural herbicides exists. Get to know your local nurseries, join plant societies, and, of course, the internet is a wealth of information on these subjects. Keeping fungus at bay was my biggest challenge with roses. I researched ways to use natural deterrents and grow my roses in harmony with the ecosystem. The fog and wind from the Pacific are real and I only managed to keep my plants healthy with natural restraints such as baking soda, Dawn Soap, or some type of oil to adhere to leaves.

It is vital to keep the area around your plants clean. Infected leaves should be tossed. Keeping gardening tools washed after pruning or contact with diseased plants is essential to avoid spreading disease. I know of a gardener who dips her pruners in bleach before moving to the next rose bush.

PLANT BEHAVIOR

If you've ever had the thrill of planting a seed and watch it puncture the soil, develop and grow into an edible vegetable or fragrant, flowering plant, you'll understand the stages of growth and development of plant behavior. As humans we begin as seeds and develop over time culminating into an employee with a lifetime of experiences that are brought to an organization. *As I watch the miraculous growth and development of my roses, the interrelationships between the multitude of systems below and above the ground that impact the development of the rose, I observe the parallels between these vast ecosystems and the world of organizations and human behavior inside the organization.*

Living in harmony with the environment or macrosystem is essential to the survival of my roses, as well as the survival of our species.

Leadership

Obviously, plants can't lead, although some would say the rapid takeover and pervasive plants occupy by aggression. However, is this leadership? Leading is the responsibility of owners who must assume this role. Leadership is not a one-person show and the most effective leaders know when, and to whom, to delegate functions.

How is it possible to understand the day-to-day needs of your rose plant if you don't look, feel, and put all your senses to work assessing what is right, wrong and favorable, evaluating all the resources needed by your precious plant and garden? Pruning helps keep roses pest free. Removing dead and spindly material shapes the plant, promotes new flowering, and ensures proper air circulation which, in turn, sets the stage for a healthy plant by preventing disease. There is a specific time of year to maximize the return on pruning—after the frost and before budding. Today, most roses are hybrid tea roses… usually pruned "hard" with an open structure for light and air.

A leader must see his or her business with a 360-degree view and "manage by walking around." Know and survey your customers, human resources and vendors. How can you lead if you never leave your office?[21]

As the owner of my garden, it is necessary for me to have knowledge to make informed decisions about care and to assess hired caretakers' output as stewards of the plants. I have a vested interest, in fact, a love and passion for my garden, and an investment of time and money toward an optimal outcome. As owner, how do I get others to buy into this same vision and outcome? What motivates others to share my values, mission and enthusiasm? Do I need to make them stakeholders in my garden's production? I do share the vegetables and bounty of flowers. Despite being paid well and working alongside them, over the long-term it might not be money alone

How can you lead if you never leave your office? How is it possible to understand the day-to-day needs of your rose plant if you don't look, feel, and put all your senses to work assessing what is right, wrong and favorable, evaluating all the resources needed by your precious plant and garden?

that motivates workers to push to do more, to take pride in their work and perform their job with the goal of excellence. In business, it is well documented that money is not the single motivator for the pursuit of quality.

Just as plants can be complemented by other plants to strengthen their growth, leaders can complement their weaknesses or augment their strengths by surrounding themselves with people who provide balance. Plants can be protective of other plants. For example, the alyssum flower attracts ladybugs and ladybugs reduce the population of harmful aphids. In a garden there is competition for resources from other plants.

In business, healthy competition can be a good thing. In the workplace are employees competing to achieve team success or is there backstabbing or undermining of others? Where does the strength of leadership begin and end?

In the garden, as in my first business, Emergency Specialist Corporation (ESC) (see Chapter 3), I learned by doing, by my successes and missteps. I spent years failing to delegate tasks, doing all the hard and heavy work which I loved. But over time, assigning tasks to others exposed me to knowledge and freed me to oversee versus micromanaging. I realized later that spending less on expert advice was actually costing me more. Being armed with knowledge was my best defense against untrustworthy vendors and helped me to balance expenses.

For years, I couldn't understand why nothing grew in a certain area of my garden. After the soil was tested, I learned excessive lime was dumped in this area during construction. I once leased four acres of my property to graze horses. The hay brought in for the horses also brought with it an invasive weed that rapidly propagated due to the nature of its roots—they developed tiny bulbs which multiplied

History is hard to shed. Short-term decisions can have long-term results. If we fail to see the cause and effect of some of our choices today, we may deal with the unintended consequences for many years to come.

aggressively, and will take years of significant energy to eradicate. History is hard to shed. Short-term decisions can have long-term results. If we fail to see the cause and effect of some of our choices today, we may deal with the unintended consequences for many years to come. (More on cause and effect in Chapter 6)

Since my garden was vast and knowledge limited, I needed help from the outset. Over the years I hired people with varying degrees of experience, and this produced a wide range of results. Some were mentors, others promised much but delivered little. The cost of untrustworthy workers was high.

In the next section, I'll discuss the significance of culture, not just in the sense of soil culture, but how the garden reflects its proprietor. Just as a business culture represents the owners with artifacts that weave the ethos of the business throughout, so will the garden's culture be visible by anyone who enters.

Culture

How do I identify a garden's culture? Just as entering a business establishment evokes certain images, so do we awaken our senses strolling the grounds of a garden. Look at its overall contents: annuals versus perennials, sun-loving versus shade and water-tolerant plants, various soil types, pest and disease resistance methods. Garden designs are strategically planned to maximize the potential of each type of plant, while allocating resources efficiently. Well-planned gardens demonstrate the culture and environment needed for each plant to thrive.

Nestled in Golden Gate Park lies the rose garden where one expects to see mulched, weeded, deadheaded, well-aligned and healthy roses. Similarly, consider the famous Butchart Gardens in Victoria, Canada; Huntington Gardens in Los Angeles; and Palm House Botanical

Gardens in Richmond, Virginia. Each plant is strategically planned considering its most suitable environment. Imagine the continual work and adjustment to keep such gardens displaying their optimal beauty. We yearn for the pleasure each flower is meant to render. We have expectations, and this is what the sometimes intangible *culture* evokes.

> *Just as a business culture represents the owners with artifacts that weave the ethos of the business throughout; so will the garden's culture be visible by anyone who enters.*

We don't press our noses to a succulent as we do a rose, nor do the billowing grass plants conjure the same effects as a stalwart dahlia flaring its plate-sized color, or the array of colorful Gerbera Daisy. If you don't think plants evoke an expected response from us you have failed to enjoy the experience of plant life, especially the flowering ones that communicate to, and with us.

Above the plant surface an orchestra of sun, wind, moisture and elements of the air gather to nourish the entire plant. Below the plant surface a subculture of tiny actors choreograph a dance to provide the plant's root nourishment: nitrogen, phosphorus, potash, calcium and magnesium. The insect soldiers are protecting the roots from intruders while worms are casting its nutrients.[22] You cannot simply feed the visible part or top of the plant organization without ensuring the root and surrounding soil are tended.

A soil's culture begins with identifying its type: sand, clay, rock, iron-rich or in desperate need of amending. The gardener tests its pH to determine if the soil is alkaline, acid or neutral, as well as if it is rich or deficient in nutrients such as nitrogen, potash, iron, micro-nutrients and so forth.

A garden's culture is represented by soil preparation, variety of plants (annuals or perennials, natives or non-natives), temperature, air quality, weather, seasonal changes, acumen of the gardener, management, history of the garden's use and structure/design/planting resources. As mentioned previously, culture is represented in a multitude of ways. How would you describe the culture of your garden? Do you believe it reflects your vision and is evident to visitors?

> *A business that fails to enrich the body of its organization will topple from a top-heavy executive staff. Just as the leaves of a tree are a microcosm of the strength of the trunk, so is the human resources a microcosm of a business organization.*

Do Plants Communicate?

Today it is widely accepted among the scientific community that plants communicate with other plants—even with plants of other species—through a complex underground network that includes the plants' rhizosphere (root ball), mycelial networks in the soil, and by emitting volatile gasses through the air. Releasing odorous chemicals called volatile organic compounds (VOCs) through the soil alerts neighbors of the many dangers they may face. In addition to warning others of herbivore attacks, the plants inform each other about threatening pathogens and impending droughts, and even recognize "family," continually adapting to the information they receive from plants growing around them.[23] These three systems work together to continuously exchange information about each plant's status.[24]

One of the organisms responsible for this amazing biochemical highway is a type of fungus called mycorrhizae.[25] These fungi form a symbiotic relationship with the plant, colonizing the roots and sending extremely fine filaments far out into the soil that act as root extensions.

We don't press our noses to a succulent as we do a rose, nor do the billowing grass plants conjure the same effects as a stalwart dahlia flaring its plate-sized color, or the array of colorful Gerbera Daisy. If you don't think plants evoke an expected response from us, you have failed to enjoy the experience of plant life, especially the flowering ones that communicate to, and with us.

Not only do these networks notify other plants about invaders, but the filaments are more effective in nutrient and water absorption than the plant roots themselves—mycorrhizae increase the nutrient absorption of the plant 100 to 1,000 times.[26]

In 2007, Susan Dudley of McMaster University in Ontario, Canada, and graduate student Amanda File showed that a beach weed called sea rocket, which is common on the shores of the Great Lakes, senses whether it's growing among siblings or unrelated plants of the same species. When a sea rocket plant detects strangers, it allocates more resources toward sprouting nutrient-grabbing roots, but when it recognizes kin, it graciously restrains itself.[27]

Companion Planting

Companion plants are said to enhance growth or protect each other from harm. Some companion plants help discourage pests without the use of chemicals because there are natural substances in their leaves, flowers, or roots that repel insects. For example, garlic, chives and ornamental alliums have been known to increase the perfume of roses,[28] ward off aphids and prevent black spot.[29] Lavender and catmint are known deterrents to rabbits. Four-o-clock and larkspur act as decoys by attracting rose-loving Japanese Beetles to eat their poisonous leaves. Yarrow attracts ladybugs; they, in turn, feed on aphids.[30]

A word of warning: *take some time to learn about the plants you place in your garden.* I planted four-o'clocks as a seed only to learn the tubers created from seed proliferate and are difficult to dig up—very, very difficult to contain. Even when I cleaved, chopped and shredded the tubers, they reappeared in my compost pile. Secondarily, this is a time to point out that some plants are toxic, in varying degrees, to animals. In your business know your employees and don't ignore the informal organization within your company (see Chapter 6).

ESTABLISHMENT

No garden is ever really established, although some of the plants, such as roses in their third-plus years, are cherished. The manicured, completely evergreen (return each year) gardens, such as rows of hedges and trees that form a landscape design, are considered established. Nothing is time-honored without hard work. The addition and removal of plants is dynamic and ongoing, as is the gardener's vision.

We feed the earth with spring bulbs in the fall to announce the onset of a new beginning, and summer bulbs in spring to ensure bursts of dahlias, peonies and more in summer. Our local nursery will always have plants in bloom for instant color satisfaction.

Gardeners even love to plant seeds in the winter, placing them inside in a variety of containers, from store-bought flats of peat moss to homemade greenhouses made out of plastic vessels or plastic bags. A variety of resources for creating such winter gardens are in books or online.

Sometimes we're captivated by the look of a single plant that elucidates a sensory response such as the peacefulness and trust of a rose, or the distrust and fear of poison oak. Many of our common plants are entirely poisonous or in part, some to humans, animals or both. A sample are: foxglove, poinsettia, lily of the valley (*Convallaria majalis)*, water hemlock *(Cicuta douglasii),* anthurium, evening nightshade (Atropa Belladonna), oleander (*Nerium oleander*), columbine *(Aquilegia)* and tobacco (*Nicotiana).*

Reflect in Your Garden

This year I removed 50 percent of my established roses. When the deer invaded, I turned my back on many cherished rose bushes for two years. The deer chewed off the tops and desecrated what had once been a garden of show-stopping, vigorous, blooming plants.

What's negative in your garden of life that needs to be removed to make space for new, positive life?

How do you face adversity when something unexpected occurs in your business or personal life?

How are you getting to know your staff better?

What are you doing to assess each employee's strengths and balancing their weaknesses with complementary staff members?

Is each staff member well matched according to skill, education and choice of position?

Is your business' vision reflected in its culture? How are customers able to experience your culture?

While all this maintenance seems like hard work, most gardeners love the time close to the roots of their passion. Keeping ahead of the S curve, as in business, is key to continued and ongoing success.

Unlike businesses today that must be relentlessly reinventing every process and product, healthy established roses are beloved. A rose does not become established or remain so without a few steadfast rules: vigilant pruning for air circulation and sucker removal, keeping the surrounding soil free of diseased leaves, ensuring the leaves remain free from fungus, immediate attention to diseases through natural means, and maintaining root moisture with a mulch and biologic nutrient amendments. For established rose plants, mulching with organic materials, like compost and shredded leaves, conserves moisture, controls weeds and keeps roots cool in summer. Spreading a two to three-inch layer of mulch around each plant, but not in direct contact with the trunk, can also help prevent the spread of diseases, such as black spot.

While all this maintenance seems like hard work, most gardeners love the time close to the roots of their passion. Keeping ahead of the curve, as in business, is key to continued and ongoing success.

Reflect in Your Garden

How much time are you spending close to the roots of your passions?

If you haven't allowed yourself time to unearth your passions and/or spend your days at a business that you love, take some time to write about what this would look like.

A business may have elements of establishment, such as a recognized logo and returning customer base, however, no business can park in the "established" lot without being towed and crushed into refuse by its competition. Businesses in the 21ˢᵗ century must constantly reinvent processes and products, remaining vigilant. You are only as successful as your next generation of products and customers.[31] A desirable garden is created with steadfast planning and execution.

MATURITY AND DECLINE

My garden of established roses blesses me with a burst of color and fragrance in June and September. Only select roses bloom all summer, just as certain businesses are cyclical. Preparation and clean-up work are constant in a garden, just as "down time" in a business signals planning, reorganizing and a different type of groundwork to ready the company. Roses cycle between a flowering and vegetative state with a transition period producing the seed-packed rosehips.[32] Ah, the miraculous interconnection between the bee pollinating the rose flower and creating a seed-filled cup called the rose hip. For the gardener, the appearance of rose hips portends the decline of the rose and the awakening of the fruit of autumn. The amber and orange-colored rose hips are the genesis of a new cycle of life bursting forth, spreading its seeds.

Few relish the wilted roses, and gardeners will remove the aged emblems of "what was" to encourage new growth. Petals of the past are returned to earth or set aside. Even a faded rose is a cherished beauty. Conjure the image of a withered rose desiccated by the sun, yet, its aroma lingers, and the wilted, wrinkled form emanates eloquence. Shall we remove the wilted leaves? We cannot restore the young buds, branches and fallen petals.

Even a Faded Rose is a Thing of Beauty

Wearing the richest red dress
wrapped in a deep green shawl
onlookers rapt by your essence

the garden's most attractive—
heads turned
a single gaze was never enough

drawn to cup your blossom
inhaling the succulent
allure of your perfume

bees gather to suckle your
sweetness—dozing into a
post-prandial somnolence

but youth is fleeting
eyes turn elsewhere
ah, beguiled by nuevo buds

the spread of
freshness opening
proved more enticing

the sun desiccates
etching your petals
into a crisp crepe

fragile but erect
I stop to reflect—
to respect

to ever cherish the
eminence of what
lingers of your perfume

Do we uproot and discard? We have too much evidence of what the corporate answer is to this question. Too often in business the matured employee is set aside. When it comes to people, maturity is a good thing—not so for a business. The tough work is maintaining what is… and timely abandon of what is obsolescent.

Stagnation results from long-term satisfaction. Sound funny? I believe this applies to both our business and personal lives. Being content for a short-term or momentarily is a wonderful feeling, however, in business you're heading toward doomsday, and personally you'll thwart your development and miss out on lots of opportunities. Change is necessary but how do you go about creating the change you desire, to design new products or services or undertake novel personal endeavors?

In the next chapter, I will introduce a process called PlanKit® that provides a nine-step pathway to create a business or personal strategic plan—*to move you from where you are to where you want to be.*

Reflect in Your Garden

What is your business' competitive advantage—what sets your company apart from the competition and other businesses?

Creating a business or planting the seed is not difficult, it's how you execute your idea and grow your business through augmenting products and staff development. How are you maximizing communication between customers and staff?

How are you providing all the resources your staff needs to complete their work?

What are you doing to enrich your personal soil, to take time for you?

This exercise is more than "reflecting" but very illuminating:

For at least one day, or better yet a week, write down how you are spending your time. Once this is done, ask yourself if you are expending your time performing the tasks that are a priority. Are you spending your time efficiently and with an opportunity for reflection?

Men who are capable of real action first make their plans and then go forward without hesitation while their enemies have still not made up their minds.

—Thucydides, *History of the Peloponnesian War*

CHAPTER 2

Analysis of Kate's Garden Using the PlanKit®

Move from where you are to where you want to be

STRATEGIC PLAN

Just as in business, a gardener should have a strategic plan that preserves what is valuable and augments what exists to create growth and sustainability. Things to contemplate are shovel pruning (getting rid of unwanted plants), adding new plants, controlling weeds and pests, pruning, weeding and amending the soil. Assess your garden in terms of what adds or detracts from its value, health and beauty. I apply the question of "opportunity cost" to decide if my time is best spent saving a poor disease-prone rose bush versus the expense of replacing it with a healthier rose breed.

PLANKIT®

To realize your goals you need to have a strategic plan. The likelihood of deviating from your goals without a strategic plan is staggering. While 80 percent of businesses survive the first year, 50 percent don't make it past year five, and of those only one in three survive 10 years. Forty percent of marriages fail, and an even greater number of unmarried couples do not remain together. A number of variables exist in the failure of a business or relationship, and an equal number of factors play a role in their success. Many individuals and businesses fail to realize their dreams or objectives because of the absence of a *plan with measurable goals and controls to keep them on track*. An anonymous source once stated, "If you fail to plan... you plan to fail." You have to want to change, as well as exert the discipline in order to see your goals to fruition.

For more than 25 years I have studied, researched and applied the concepts of organizational theory as a business consultant and professor. With each business consulting assignment I garnered fresh wisdom to problem solve; when teaching graduate students how to analyze businesses, I uncovered newfound revelations with each course. These epiphanies led me to create a process to assist clients in developing a strategic plan, as well as a methodology to successfully execute it. As more and more clients came to me expressing gratitude for their brand-new direction resulting from using the process, I created PlanKit®.

> *PlanKit® is a process to move you from where you are to where you want to be...*

PlanKit® is a nine-step process that applies business tools and theories that I simplified so that any individual, business, entrepreneur or anyone in a relationship (family, marriage, or teams) can utilize to build a strategic plan. Utilizing the PlanKit® you'll be presented with a step-wise process to create an organizational or personal strategic plan—where you envision your business or personal life in the future.

The PlanKit® includes Kurt Lewin's Model of Change, gap analysis, identifying your strengths, weaknesses, opportunities and threats (SWOT) analysis, identifying your core values and goals, Lewin's Force Field Analysis (FFA), cause and effect diagram, balancing and reinforcing causal loops and Porter's Model of Five Forces. Two of the tools, the Force Field Analysis (FFA) and cause and effect diagram, are problem-solving instruments intended to help you drill down to the root cause of why you are not arriving at your destination and provide you with a methodology to put you back on course.

The theories and models behind the nine-step process in PlanKit® have a mathematical and/or scientific derivation, and have been transferred to or adopted by other disciplines—such as business and psychology—just as I have selected and packaged such theories into the process of PlanKit®.

> *If you don't control your own destiny someone else will.*
>
> ~Jack Welch

This process is a roadmap to a business strategic plan and a personal GPS to achieve your goals. Creating the plan is only the first step; the real work is just beginning. Your success is dependent on the measurable controls you put in place, as well as paying attention to data your controls reveal. I come from a healthcare background where the sound of alarms are ubiquitous. "Alarm creep" is a well-documented syndrome that leads those who respond to endless alarms to begin to ignore them. The downfalls are obvious—ignoring data will eventually lead to discounting important information.

Nine Steps of PlanKit®

Step 1—Model of Change

The first of the nine-step process is you have to *want to change*, according to Kurt Lewin's Model of Change, a simple concept that consists of three parts, unfreezing, change and refreezing. As long as I held onto an old way of viewing my garden, change would not occur. In order to realize the garden I now envisioned, it was necessary for me to unfreeze previous thinking; to share my vision of expanding the existing garden with those that would help me see the newly designed half-acre to fruition. Once we make a shift in our thinking, or the action of *unfreezing*, we progress to the second part in the 3-part change model—*create the change*. I moved through the transition of rethinking and creating the vision, to establish a new, expanded garden. The third step of *refreezing* will occur when the garden is established and extolling its gifts of natural beauty, gracing me and all who visit.[33]

> *Change before you have to...*
>
> ~Jack Welch

Step 2—Gap Analysis

The second step in the PlanKit® process is to envision *where you are today and where you want to be in the future*; in business this procedure is called a gap analysis. How did I envision my garden from the established, one-acre space I had tended for 15 years, to create an expanded place of solace designed to honor my father, to pay him and his poetry homage through the life and poetry of my garden? How could I honor nature through the poetic theme my dad weaved throughout our lives? After dad passed, one of my clients arrived at my home with a 20-gallon, purple hibiscus tree. I told him it would forever be my *poetree*. It remains vibrant and dresses the entrance gate to my home.

Another kind of gap existed after my dad's passing— the void within my heart. Embellishing my view with roses, dahlias, fresh veggies, and more, not only framed my home with natural beauty, but, as I kneaded soil, pulled weeds and planted new life, my garden gave me the opportunity to fill the vacant pockets of my heart.

My heart would never fully heal after I lost my father, but I feel his spirit when in the garden. I've no doubt he's present as each season spreads its flora across Mother Nature's table for me to share with so many. My flowers have adorned wedding tables, birthday parties, an array of special occasions and into the homes of many. Not only did I move from where I was to where I wanted to be, but harvested joy with each bouquet.

Reflect In Your Garden

The following questions refer to your business, personally, or both.

Contemplate where you are versus where you want to be.

Identify at least one aspect of your business or one part of your daily life you want to change.

What makes you believe you are ready to change?

Step 3—Core Values: Tenets You Will Not Compromise

An examination of your core values and/or the core values of your business is the third step in the PlanKit® process. My most closely held core value related to my garden was being a good steward of the land, keeping it one with the environment. Consequently, I did everything in my power to maintain the natural habitat of the land while preserving my vision of expanding the garden. I wanted to expand my knowledge, too, as I considered information my best friend and companion. In order to realize my vision, I needed to know the most effective natural herbicides and insecticides, efficient but natural gopher control, drought-resistant and resource-preserving plants—all to keep homeostasis of nature's resources while enjoying the beauty of my garden. How could I preserve and respect Mother Nature as I met the many challenges of working with the land?

I only wanted to utilize natural means of gopher and rodent control. As mentioned earlier, I tried everything from noise vibrations to smelly socks. I did take preventative measures to keep the gophers away from my plants' roots by wrapping them in wire baskets. Unfortunately, I found myself in a daytime nightmare surrounded by a band of gophers peering out of their holes mocking me.

In Step 7, you will be introduced to the concept of cause and effect within a system and unintended consequences. I offer the case of my kitten rescue: For a few years I rescued kittens, fostering a temporary home for litters until matched with suitable homes. With each litter I nurtured, one of the kittens would steal my heart. The unintended consequence—I amassed a crew of eight protective cat soldiers standing ready to keep the gophers at bay.

In business, owners must be cognizant of their impact on the environment. Every business owner must be a responsible curator, contributing positively to their surroundings. Such stewardship includes benevolence through charitable contributions and policies to reduce any negative impact on the physical environment. Companies such as Patagonia are an example of environmental stewardship, weaving a vision of themselves as nature's custodians while appealing to customers who share their mission. An excerpt from Patagonia's mission statement follows:[34] (See also section on Leadership)

> *We donate our time, services and at least one percent of our sales to help hundreds of grassroots organizations all over the world so that they can remain vigilant, and protect what's irreplaceable. At the same time, we know that we risk saving a tree only to lose the forest—a livable planet.*

Unequivocally, time in the garden nourishes my soul. The solace my garden provides is greatly cherished. Simply crossing the threshold of my home, leaving behind my daily challenges and entering the fragrance of green, I'm wrapped in calm. When gardening, I only listen to the natural sounds encircling me: the nearby ocean, a choir of birds, the screeching of the hawks, and the clamoring of the palm fronds.

STEP 4—SWOT ANALYSIS

A SWOT is a simple business tool, an uncensored inventory by an individual or group of the strengths, weaknesses, opportunities and threats within a system. In this case I am using the SWOT to analyze the internal strengths and weaknesses and external opportunities and threats of my garden circa 2007 (see table). The flat topography and approximate half-acre, square parcel, leant itself to open access for deliveries and service trucks, which would be necessary for soil and material delivery. In general, the unobstructed space allowed for the summoning of a design of my choosing. After the irrigation and infrastructure were installed, 200 yards of soil were delivered, rolled flat, and half was seeded as lawn. The remainder was poured and spread into the three separate spaces that I had designed to contain the different sections of my garden.

The sandy soil was a strength, as it is permeable and porous for good drainage. Creating three segregated spaces allowed for different watering and soil needs in each section. For example, I chose to hand water the roses to avoid fungus caused by too much moisture and overhead watering. I have a well with large storage tanks, allowing me to have a rose garden when drought seemed unending. The privacy of my property keeps human intruders from destroying plants. Unfortunately, gophers, and the expanding deer population, multiple rodents, rose-destroying insects and disease are weaknesses and an incessant battle.

SWOT Analysis of Kate's Garden – An Inventory of Strengths, Weaknesses, Opportunities and Threats

STRENGTHS	WEAKNESSES
Sandy soil / ocean climate	Insects (can be strength depending on type)
Passionate gardener; always seeking new information to enhance my garden	Limited experience in garden design/knowledge
Love of nature and drawn to be close to nature	Gophers, rabbits, moles
Five acres with acre landscaped, easy access for deliveries, surrounded by state-owned land	Proximity of the garden to the ocean and marine layer
Segregated spaces to accommodate the separate needs of the plants contained in each space	Disease; the time it takes to control; challenge of growing roses near the ocean
Underground watering system/ well	Propagation of deer (may be a threat also)
OPPORTUNITIES	THREATS
Make my flowers available to many	Excessive cost of labor
Feed the bees, insects, contribute to ecosystem	County regulations limiting what I can grow
Expand into a vegetable or commercial garden on additional four acres	Rural environment and surrounding invasive weeds with years of propagation
Possibility of leasing land to strawberry or other growers	Fog and introduction to disease Need for more water to support leased/external growing community

Both an opportunity and threat were the garden's proximity to the ocean and exposure to the marine layer and fog. This layer controlled the variation in temperature of approximately 20 degrees, as it never got too hot or too cold. Fruit trees and plants that needed a cold winter, such as gardenias, would bloom once but not likely in the following years. Corn grew into stalks but no actual cob was produced due to the lack of constant heat.

Now that I had an inventory of the strengths and weaknesses of my garden, I created a plan to balance both sides of the equation. The sandy soil was amended by adding mulch and compost. Sun and shade-loving plants were placed strategically for optimal health.

To complement the weaknesses and mitigate risks, aviary wire was double-layered in each flower bed, organic products like wood chips and newspaper were applied to reduce the growth of weeds, and my eight cats kept the gopher population down. I introduced beneficial insects to ameliorate negative pests and, after studying marine-loving plants, began filling the beds with hydrangeas, rock roses, salvias and an array of suitable bulbs.

The opportunity existed to extend the garden beyond its current perimeter. Only one of the five acres was purposefully planted. The other four acres could be leased to nearby farmers, yet my privacy and water source was of concern. I had the opportunity to grow a splendid vegetable garden, but too many crops could make it more labor intensive if I wasn't going to sell at the farmer's market. Threats were abundant: wind blowing nearby weed seeds and the beating of salt air into plants, plus drought and fog. I realized the more complex the garden, the more diligence and continuous oversight was necessary. Daily watering and observation of the soil, minor pruning, deadheading, weeding and eliminating self-seeding plants were part of the day-to-day routine.

Like complex gardens, complex organizations necessitate acute diligence and oversight. One must be ever cognizant to complement weaknesses with resources and maximize the strengths of a company. For example, no leader possesses all the qualities to effectively carry out his/her vision. An astute leader does not surround themselves with clones, but knows how to leverage their strong points and counter their weak points. Most companies diversify their products, sometimes seasonally, or into different sectors, to lessen the exposure to risk. The key strategy is to know the business, listen to feedback and maintain balance. Getting out of the office and walking around to observe day-to-day work so as to take the needed action to maintain stability is a must for a successful business.

A leader must also be ever vigilant to external threats and competition. Remember, opportunities and threats are external to the business. A single regulation or increase in costs, can create instability that must be overcome with increased revenue. I'm doubtful that a pandemic was ever on the threats side of the equation. For some companies, the pandemic was an opportunity to sell online and a plethora of new businesses, or reconfiguring an existing business, have arisen as a result of shifting a threat into an opportunity. In turn, individuals have seized what may have first appeared as a threat and turned it into an opportunity.

STEP 5—GOALS AND OBJECTIVES: USING A QUANTIFIABLE APPROACH

You must not only identify *measurable* short, medium and long-term goals, but do so in a detailed manner with quantifiable measurements. This ensures accountability to guarantee you will achieve your desired outcome.

My *short-term goals for the garden overall*, to be completed in *a year's time* (second year) were to keep the garden rid of reseeding plants, weeds, gophers, unwanted insects and disease.

Mid-term goals, to be completed within *years three to five*, were to expand to a vegetable garden to give produce to friends, and have fresh, organic food for myself. I would plant iceberg, radicchio, red leaf and arugula greens. Additionally, I would plant carrots, tomatoes, cilantro and green onions. Move from only mini-roses to healthy, fragrant and hybridized for the best of both old roses and hybrid teas. Fill my rose garden with David Austin bred roses.

Long-term goals, to complete within *ten years*, were to do research on companion planting and put my knowledge to work to increase yield while decreasing insects, weeds and disease.

Step five in PlanKit® asks you to create a list of goals and detailed steps to attain each of the goals. For example, in order to achieve one of my short-term goals it was necessary to undertake a study of disease-resistant roses.

I delineate a few steps needed to meet my goal:

1. Take a class on rose growing for the home gardener at the community college during winter semester this year.

2. Renew memberships with Monterey and San Francisco Rose Societies and consult Rosarians.

3. Talk to other rose growers in my area, including plant nurseries.

4. Do a comprehensive online search to find the best books on rose growing and natives.

5. Load applications that identify plants and maintenance instructions.

All these actions were methods of maintaining checks and balances.

Goals Must Be Measurable

What's wrong with the short-term goals above? What are the milestones and measurable objectives? Are there dates to plant, a calendar of optimal times for pruning and transplanting? How do we know the plants are thriving, and what controls are in place to ensure the plants are on a sustainable path? What homework needs to be done before undertaking a garden expansion, and, most importantly, what are the ideal plants for my climate?

Let's move from general gardening goals to an example of a more detailed description of identifying a goal and how to meet it.

Growing a Beautiful Rose

I had been trying to reach the goal of growing a beautiful rose for several years. It has been difficult getting to the root cause of my failure, simply because the goal was too broad. What do I mean by the statement, *a beautiful rose*? One can see this statement is subjective and difficult to break down into measurable variables. However, I could set my goal more precisely *to grow a disease-free rose by spring of 2022*. The narrower and more defined a goal, the more likely we are to meet it, and a clearly defined goal is easier to measure as well. At this point, let's define my goal as: *grow a red, hybrid tea, floribunda rose, free of black spot, rust and powdery mildew by April of 2022*. Now, I am far more likely to reach this goal because I have limited the scope in terms of input: *red, hybrid tea, floribunda* and more measurable output: *free of black spot, rust* and *powdery mildew*. I have now narrowed my search of the type of plant I need, realizing that each of the aforementioned diseases are a kind of fungus and each can be from different spores.

Reflect in Your Garden

(The questions below can refer to your business, personally or both)

Create your SWOT. Simply take a plain piece of paper and draw a large plus sign (+). Label the upper quadrants with Strength and Weakness and the lower two quadrants with Opportunities and Threats. Remember: the strengths and weaknesses are internal and opportunities and threats are external to you or your business. (See example)

How will you complement the weaknesses and leverage your strengths?

Make a list of the goals you want to achieve in one year, five years and ten years.

Next, detail how you will achieve each of your goals, including a means for measuring the progress toward completing the goal.

What controls/measurements will you use to determine if you're meeting the goals of your garden, or life?

❧

STEP 6—FORCE FIELD ANALYSIS: WHY IS YOUR GOAL NOT BEING MET?

Goals can be complex. Natural forces either drive us toward or restrain us from meeting our goals, according to Kurt Lewin,[35] an organizational theorist. Lewin created the force field analysis (FFA) as a tool to explore the push and pull, toward and away, from reaching our goals (see Chapter 6). Let's look at the goal of eradicating pervasive intruders such as weeds, rodents and plant diseases in my garden. I can easily make a list of the driving and restraining forces that are at play as I attempt to reach my objectives. Lewin identifies "driving forces" toward change and counter "resisting forces" away from change while striving for balance or homeostasis. *Remember, driving and restraining forces are the energies that are in opposition. Our work is to reduce the strength and number of restraining forces and increase the strength and number of driving forces.* (See more on homeostasis in Chapters 5 & 6).

The restraining forces that keep me from having the well-manicured, healthy garden seem endless. There is nothing more challenging, time-consuming, and that wreaks havoc on my plants' nutrients, than weeds. In my garden there is a war for nutrients and space being played out constantly between strategically placed plants and voluntary weeds. Additionally, rodents uproot and destroy flowering plant roots and the fog, salt and wind from the marine weather causes plant diseases. Are the number and strengths of the driving forces greater than those inhibiting me from the flowering sanctuary I desire? Consult the chart that follows on the next page:

First, identify restraining forces, those forces that keep you from reaching a goal. Then brainstorm the driving forces pushing you toward your goal. In the example below the goal is to create a beautiful flower garden in honor of my dad.

DRIVING FORCES	RESTRAINING FORCES
Passion for gardening and roses	Gophers and rodents
Willing to do the work required	Cost
Good soil, sufficient land	Work to maintain a landscaped acre
Campaign to eradicate negative intrusions	Weather such as drought and fog
The legacy to honor my dad	Insects and disease
Knowledge of growing roses/ flowers	Weeds
Being close to nature and God, a sanctuary that calms me	Overcome the long-term effects of my garden's location in a cool, salty, marine, coastal environment
TOTAL	TOTAL

After identifying driving and restraining forces, *I assigned a number associated with the strength or weakness of a force, with 1 being the weakest and 5 the strongest force.*

DRIVING FORCES		RESTRAINING FORCES	
Passion for gardening and roses	5	Gophers and rodents	4
Willing to do the work required	4	Cost	3
Good soil, sufficient land	2	Work to maintain a landscaped acre	4
Campaign to eradicate negative intrusions	3	Weather such as drought and fog	4
The legacy to honor my dad	5	Insects and disease	5
Knowledge of growing roses/ flowers	3	Weeds	5
Being close to nature and God, a sanctuary that calms me	5	Overcome the long-term effects of my garden's location in a cool, salty, marine, coastal environment	4
TOTAL	27	TOTAL	29

Keep in mind the assignment of a force's strength or weakness is subjective based on the individual or group's sentiment, attitudes and opinions. Considering both driving and restraining forces, we know these forces are in opposition. We have to reduce the strong restraining forces or increase the driving forces or both.

So, how do you reduce the strong restraining forces? First, you have to get to the root causes of the powerful effects on the beautiful garden you want to create. What if you want to reduce the strong forces keeping you from meeting your goals? Again, you must identify the causes, and eventually the root causes, of what is creating the powerful effect.

Using my garden as an example, let's undertake Step Six in PlanKit® to get to the root causes of the strong restraining forces identified above— the effects of the intrusion of weeds and disease/insects.

STEP 7—CAUSE AND EFFECT

Because I used overhead watering of my roses, versus hand watering or drip irrigation directly watering at the roots, I created an *effect* of fungus and weed intrusion. How do I eradicate the fungus and lower the intrusion of weeds, by identifying potential causes: too much moisture left on rose plants, failure to eradicate before seeding, not weeding, and underground rodents carrying seeds? Use this equation in your own examination: Because I did X (Cause) then Y (Effect) occurred.

The first action to take in this cause and effect exercise is to identify one of the items with a strong force and/or 5 in the above example of my force field analysis: the "abatement of weeds" or "depletion of all intruders" of the garden.

Keep asking "why" questions to get to the root of the problem. Why are insects and disease invading my roses? Perhaps it's because I'm overwatering. **Why** are you overwatering? I water overhead versus hand water. **Why** not hand water? It takes too much time. **Why** are you spending so much time hand watering? Each plant needs to be individually watered close to the roots. **Why** individually water? So the rose plant doesn't get diseased from water on the leaves. Then **why** are you watering overhead versus finding a way to install a system that waters close to the roots? The cost is too high to replace the irrigation system. **Why** isn't the cost of drip irrigation worth the cost of replacing beautiful roses or managing the disease, as well as your time spent watering?

This may be a silly example but one that, if given the opportunity to unearth the root cause, solves the problem long-term. I assure you the really tough original causes to uncover are those that implicate a vice president of a company, or admitting a product is a failure.

To determine the root cause of a problem, look at every part of the system and the interrelationships between the parts of the system.

In companies and relationships, getting to the source cause can be threatening because of the action we have to take to make change. It's less disruptive to create work-arounds or throw more money at a lagging product just to appease its developer. In Chapter 6 we will discuss a number of common organizational dysfunctions that keep us from dealing with the core of an issue.

Maybe the original cause is simply because we want something and accept the challenges it represents. Let's examine the "restraining force" of fungus as a result of the foggy climate. **Why** is there so much fungus growing on my roses? Since I live in a foggy climate and I want to grow roses, I cannot eradicate all disease. So, **why** do you grow roses in a foggy climate? Because I love roses and I simply want to have a rose garden and will accept a less perfect rose bush or spend a bit more money for hybridized roses that are hardier and healthier. Sometimes we just need to learn how to reduce the restraining forces—to best eradicate garden intruders. I can at least create barriers (like wearing a raincoat in a storm). I can move my roses to the sunniest location, apply a simple soap solution, use natural fungicides and insecticides, and bring in ladybugs to combat aphids.

How do I lower the intrusion of weeds (the effect)? I might have to sacrifice time, by hand weeding more often; or money, by having a gardening service mitigate the problem with weekly visits. Additionally, I could gain knowledge by undertaking a study of the ingenious ways organic growers have developed to take care of pesky unwanted plants. For instance, carpeting the ground with newspaper, mulching around plants, or spreading a concoction of corn gluten meal to prevent germination. I drove by a tree cutting service taking down a row of pine trees. They were only too happy to deliver the wood chips to my home. Of course, I paid to have the chips spread but saved hundreds of dollars not having to purchase 50 yards of wood chips.

Roses need a lot of water, but how do you determine when a rose needs watering, especially when living in a foggy climate? I decided to use a gauge to determine soil moisture. *When trying to determine the root cause of a problem, look at every part of the system and the interrelationships between the parts of the system.*

Excessive water on and around rose plants is just one of the many causes leading to the effects of weed seeds germinating, certain insects harboring and coastal winds creating the ideal medium for fungus to propagate. Arming ourselves with knowledge and continuously learning are excellent ways to become good stewards of our gardens and businesses. When solving a problem in any organization, from gardens to companies, you must know all the parts within the organization, but, *more importantly, understand the interrelationships between the parts.* How systems interrelate is at the core of systems theory. I write extensively on systems theory in Chapter 5, but I want to introduce the concept here to provide you with a foundation for understanding the importance of the next step in PlanKit®.

STEP 8—BALANCING AND REINFORCING CAUSAL LOOPS

In the course of a day, consider the innumerable adjustments you make in the infinite systems you encounter. When I'm thirsty I drink water, but how much? Driving my car I adjust the speed dozens of times depending on what I encounter. If I want a warmer shower or hotter soup I adjust the nozzle or change the gas burner to reach just the right temperature. How much time can I subtract from my meeting in order to get to my daughter's soccer game? An Olympic medalists wins by shaving hundreds of a second off her time. How? How do you adjust for poor reviews, negative cash flow, high vacancy rates or a growing employee turnover rate in your business?

One thing many of us struggle with is balancing our lives. How do I change today in order to get what I want tomorrow?

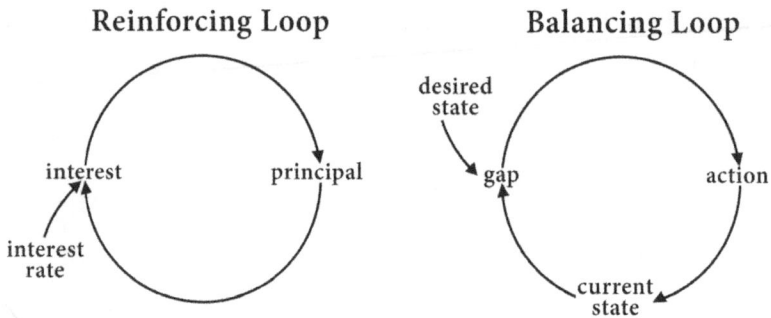

Reinforcing Loop

interest

interest rate

principal

Balancing Loop

desired state

gap

current state

action

A balancing loop is considered a "negative" loop because it pushes back on a "doing the same thing over and over," routine or process otherwise known as a reinforcing loop. Balancing and reinforcing loops are the show stoppers, the big kahunas, that pull all the prior seven steps of PlanKit® together. In the first step, we ask the question of whether we are ready for change? In Step 2, we must describe our current situation and the vision we foresee in the future—to move from where we are to where we want to be. Step 3 asks us to inventory our strengths, weaknesses, opportunities and threats in order to complement our weaknesses, leverage our strengths and mitigate threats while maximizing on the opportunities. In Step 4 you determine if your values are aligned with the business you started or how you choose to spend most of your time. At every step we are incrementally moving to disrupt our current status and determine what it is we need to do to rebalance. Some call this a "tipping point" that sets in motion a significant life change such as starting a business, going back to school, getting married or retiring. Or, this cycle can represent continuous change in order to streamline processes, create new products or reinvesting to improve financially. We are aborting the cycle of linear thought to one of questioning and on to action.

Step 5 is the most important and difficult step as we lay out detailed goals and milestones to arrive at "where we want to be." Balancing loops adjust input in order to arrive at the desired output. Balancing and reinforcing loops represent the push and pull between the restraining and driving forces of Step 6.

I introduce balancing and reinforcing loops to demonstrate how to problem solve using the basic system diagram that follows.

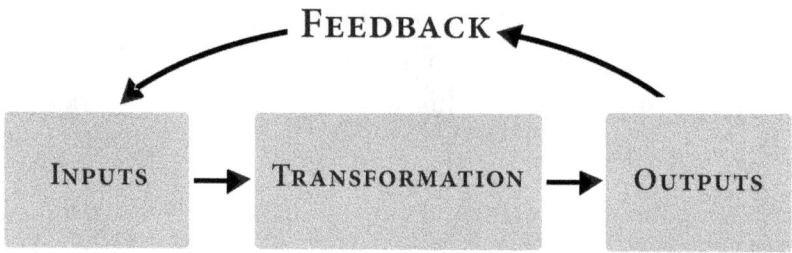

Simply stated, every system has *inputs*, that are *transformed* into *outputs*, and continuous *feedback* to keep the system in balance.[36]

Applying this simple description of a system to my garden: seeds as inputs being transformed with water, nutrients, energy into the output, a plant. Now, let's consider the intrusion of gophers or weeds as a problem at the *input or transformation phase* of the system, and impacting the *output* portion of the system. How will you change the input to influence the output? Remember, energy must be expended to keep the system in balance. How did I know what the problem was until I witnessed the disappearance of the plant being sucked under by a gopher, or observed a wilting, dying, tipped plant with sinking soil beneath my feet? The *feedback,* visual evidence, was not seen in the first year of growth in my garden which was prepped with two layers of aviary wire crisscrossed over the entire circle and enclosed in stucco. Such reinforcements were strong deterrents to any intruders, and no weed seeds had a chance to find a home in my new garden.

The second year, I found the new roses I had planted uprooted, leaves turning under, spots appearing on the leaves that blemished the previous year's brilliant green. Not only had the gophers found a way to bypass the aviary wire, and the fog marred my shiny green leaves leaving fungus and, a new virulent group of pests descended on my plants. I now looked at weeds with new curiosity. I wanted to know their names, when they appeared, and how they were seeded into my space. Without this knowledge how could I begin to naturally eradicate them? I did not want to wait until the weeds appeared and competed with my splendid output; I wanted to proactively mitigate the risk before spending time and money getting rid of these intruders. Birds and wind spread seeds as do underground vermin dropping weed seeds along their subterranean paths. What else could I have done to be proactive?

I failed to anticipate, to navigate, and scan every possible source of competition. What didn't I do at the input phase to anticipate problems at the transformation and output phases? Is the cause at the input, transformation or output portion of the system? How will you change the input to impact the output?

My illustrations of balancing and reinforcing loops are intentionally simple, although in reality even simple systems are ever changing. Balancing loops illustrate homeostasis, introducing variables that return, in this case, the plant to equilibrium.[37] For example, drought can be balanced by water retention processes such as mulch, or let nature work her miracle of growing roots deeper. In any open system, of which nature is a quintessential example, change is incessant and the system works hard to adjust. To maintain health, a system will seek internal methods to alter input or output to sustain balance. As Lady Justice represents balance of evidence, so do plant systems and our macro ecosystem look for stability. Gardeners, like business people, inadvertently upset nature's balance by negatively altering the environment within which they work— for example, the application of chemicals into the soil and air. There is a natural depletion of needed resources and some plants rob nutrients from nearby plants.

Too often solutions are ineffective because we have not uncovered the root of the problem. I've seen more misplaced resources expended due to knee-jerk, quick-fix solutions employed by managers answering to a crew of nipping dogs at their ankles. It's like shoving a nipple into the mouth of a crying child instead of taking the time to uncover the real cause of the problem. Why is getting to the root of a problem so difficult? Not only is it time intensive, but doing so may be too uncomfortable to reveal. Uncovering the root cause means having to address the real problem, oftentimes, with a difficult solution. For example, an ineffective manager was the reason for staff turnover, frequent sick calls, complaints to owners, which eventually impacted customer satisfaction. The owners hired a consultant to intervene rather than fire the long-term employee. An executive confessed to me that consultants were brought in to temporarily run the company due to the fact that, despite knowing what was needed to save the company, the executive staff was *just too close to the problems to effect the necessary changes needed.* Let's take a look at another example of cause and effect and balancing and reinforcing loops.

I was consulting for a community hospital's administration to advise if staffing complements were adequate over 24 hours in its emergency department. I interviewed all staff on all shifts. One registered nurse on the night shift spent more time than any of the others fault-finding about the *lack of staff.* She shared that this was not the only hospital where she worked and how other emergency departments were comparatively staffed with *sometimes two to three times the number of nurses* relative to the emergency department we were standing in. An hour later, she was sitting at the nurses' station flanked by three other nurses laughing at photos of her recent vacation.

The very nurse who complained that "a lack of staff was at the root of overworked staff in the emergency department," in fact, had time to watch videos with the entire staff while at work— irrespective of their duties as nurses, ignoring their responsibility to the hospital to care for patients and remain alert to the needs of the department while at work. Obviously, the root cause of ineffective nursing care was not a lack of staff but a lack of responsible staff. Unless the decision makers are present to observe the real causes of ineffective nursing care, more staff may be the answer to the "effect" of inadequate nursing care.

Another factor that is often overlooked in such circumstances is the power of group dynamics that creates a misunderstanding over what is at the root of inefficient care. There is a good deal of documentation that suggests individuals are influenced more by belonging to

PlanKit® *is a nine-step process that applies business tools and theories that I simplified so that any individual, business, entrepreneur or anyone in a relationship (family, marriage, or teams) can utilize to build a strategic plan—a process to move you from where you are to where you want to be.*

a group than doing the right thing. In other words, an individual would succumb to performing at a sub-par level rather than stand out as a top performer in order to be accepted by the group. This is an example of the "informal" organization being as, or more, powerful as the "formal" organization. So why do I address the topics of group dynamics and informal organizations in a discussion of cause and effect? Because, organizations too often throw resources at a problem rather than drill down to the less tangible, complex "interrelationships" that contribute to an issue. In Chapters 5 and 6 I will discuss systems theory and group dynamics further.

As we move to the final step in PlanKit® please remember this is an exercise to perform a retrospective analysis of the design and establishment of the garden I dedicated to my dad using the PlanKit® process. Mother Nature is a great teacher. The PlanKit® process provides business tools for reflection and to create change in your business and personal life.

I devised PlanKit® for any individual or business owner to apply the steps toward analyzing oneself and/or company, leading to a strategic plan. Moving to the final step in PlanKit®, I will discuss Porter's Model of Five Forces, developed by Michael Porter, considered one of the world's authorities on strategy.

Bargaining Power of Buyers	Bargaining Power of Suppliers
Competitors in the Industry	
Threat of Substitution	Threat of New Entrants

Step 9—Porter's Model of Five Forces

In 1979 Michael Porter, educated in aerospace engineering, business and economics, developed Porter's Model of Five Forces.[38] The Model is the *sine qua non* for a business to track the external environment for competition so as to refine, redesign and reinvent products and processes to improve profitability. Imperative to the application of Porter's Model of Five Forces is the analysis of significant threats against your business' profitability. Let's take a closer look at the five forces impacting the profitability of competing businesses within an industry: bargaining power of buyers, bargaining power of suppliers, threat of new entrants, threat of substitute products or services. At the core of the model is competition within the industry.

Bargaining Power of Buyers

I'm sure you have all heard the adage "it's a buyer's market," and what better example than the real estate crash of 2007, flooding the housing industry with a glut of foreclosed properties. In recent years the trend has shifted to a seller's market due to low interest rates, the rising cost of building materials and a demand for investment properties. Flipping homes and vacation rental trends are intensifying demand and low inventory. While not necessarily in direct proportion, typically an inverse relationship exists between low interest rates and high real estate prices. When interest rates were double digit in the 1970s and 80s prices dropped, the inventory of homes grew, days on market increased and sellers were desperate, driving prices down. The root cause of such complex systems problems is most likely the result of government policy makers.

So what companies are in competition for the profits in real estate? Agents, lenders, brokers, architects, developers, builders and all the inspectors who ensure the salability of the property. Also, consider all the retailers who create the pieces of real estate infrastructure such as appliances and cabinets. There is very little differentiation, or ownership, in the top real estate agencies.

Bigger is better when it comes to bargaining power. This fact is why hundreds of doctors have joined together, partnering with hospital systems, in order to negotiate better reimbursement rates with insurance companies. Obviously, warehouse chains like Costco, Sam's Club and Home Depot can negotiate more deeply discounted prices from vendors than smaller, less diversified stores. Amazon is an oligopoly that capitalized on the power of the internet and took collaboration to a whole new level. Take a moment to consider all the companies that have integrated for buying power.

Bargaining Power of Suppliers

Control over the "inputs" by suppliers is one way to "disrupt" the supply chain and impact an industry's profitability. A supply chain consists of suppliers, manufacturers, warehouses, distribution centers and then on to retailers. Any disruption along the supply chain will create demand by the retailers and its customers. McDonald's held the number one spot in supply chain management until Amazon displaced them into the number two spot. McDonald's has a vertically integrated system that efficiently manages a small group of suppliers bound by a value-based strategy of an "inter-dependent partnership" with shared profits between suppliers and franchise owners.[39] Another example of a vertically integrated business is the Kaiser Permanente healthcare provider. Kaiser is known for its "cradle-to-grave" delivery system. A vertically integrated business technically provides all the services a customer needs—in the case of Kaiser, this includes an insurance provider.

Sam Walton was known for strategically placing his distribution centers to shorten the time spent getting product to Walmart, followed by the arrival of the warehouse stores that cut costs by selling directly to customers and eliminating the cost of moving product to retail stores.

Frangibility of Supply and Demand

As of this writing in July 2021, supply chain shortages, exacerbated by the COVID-19 pandemic, are creating a "supply and demand" dilemma. For purposes of illustrating the use of Porter's Model I'm going to focus on two particular shortages, the silicon chip [industry] and lumber [production]. The backlogs are impacting a broad reach of businesses from construction to microwaves to paper goods. In such complex systems, as these industries exemplify, every part is interconnected resulting in a series of causes and effects.[40]

In both cases the supply shortages have resulted from a convergence of events. Looking first at the shortage of silicon chips—the data suggests the main cause is a failure to plan. Most of the chip production is done in Asia and a lack of investment into the growth of chip manufacturing appears to be at the root of the problem. Other factors range from sanctions on China , the temporary closure of chip plants in Texas due to an unprecedented winter freeze, a fire in a Japanese chip plant and aggressive buying by the big cell phone producers, Apple and Samsung, to ensure the rollout of their 5G phones.

Families ordered to stay home due to COVID-19, created an unexpected rise in the use of cell phones and personal computers for work and school—and, of course, gaming devices. At the same time, General Motors cancelled orders for cars when COVID-19 hit, however, online sales caused an uptick in the demand for automobiles as people craved a bit of freedom. When the automakers resumed production, manufacturing could not keep up with the demand due to the lack of semiconductors. Tens of thousands of vehicles are now parked on lots waiting for the backlogged chips before delivery of cars can resume.

Initially the shortage appeared to only impact the auto industry, however, the chip shortage will be far-reaching and economists predict that the scarcities will impact the availability of commodities beyond Christmas 2021.[41] In fact, today's estimates indicate probable shortages into 2023 on some products. Elaborating on the significance of a broken supply chain on the profitability of an industry, the semiconductor shortage is estimated to cost the global auto industry $110 billion in revenue.[42] This is today's estimate.

Wood Shortages

Once again, a confluence of events have culminated in the exponential rise in the cost of lumber. Plywood has soared to four times that of the previous year's price. Fires across the world have decreased the supply of wood, adding to existing shortages caused by the ecology minded who have thwarted the milling of trees. The cost of lumber production has increased due to a limited wood supply that has resulted from bans on deforestation. Home remodeling during and after the pandemic has caused a boom in manufacturing that has given rise to a demand for lumber. Not only is lumber in demand, but the rising costs of wood byproducts are also due to the rise in gas and labor costs. The abrupt closure of the Keystone Pipeline has resulted in a 40 percent spike in gas prices in a single year—with transportation costs passed on to consumers. Kimberly Clark has increased the cost of toilet paper products by 20 percent.[43]

Threat of Substitute Products and Services

Continuing the discussion of wood and semiconductor chip shortages as of July 2021, how long will buyers wait for the products they need if months of delay in procuring lumber impact the cost or feasibility to build or remodel a home? The homeowner may decide that hardwood floors can be replaced by stone or tile. Some manufacturers of small appliances and automobile orders have extended delivery dates into next year. A paper supply shortage may be mitigated by the use of digital devices. For paper products such as paper towels and toilet tissue, some rationing may need to be put in place such as was implemented at the peak of the pandemic in 2020.

In actuality, paper as a medium for reading has diminished significantly in the past 15-plus years—from phone books to newspapers as well as digital formats for reading novels and textbooks. Paper media companies had to adapt or die. Newspapers and magazines now deliver their content online and books are moving to a predominately digitized medium. To ensure a revenue stream, fee-based subscriptions for use of the digital mediums are typically required. Substitutes or new entrants into an industry is a force against profitability.

Commercial business locations are being supplanted by online storefronts and mega warehouse retailers; one or two choices of chain pharmacies or superstores such as CVS and Target have rendered small or single specialty stores nearly obsolete. Homegrown retailers have emerged in the online retail spaces of Etsy, Ebay and Amazon.

What makes the threat of substitution high or low? Ask yourself if the barrier to entry into your market is high or low, or is the ease and cost to switch, time and cost beneficial? Online retailers have created the greatest chaos when we consider new entrants in a traditional marketplace. The short-distance ground transportation system has been upset by Uber. Cafeteria style streaming services and smart TVs have responded to a demand from consumers who want more choice and less cost. Incubator kitchens that prepare food for delivery-only are meeting customer demands at a lower cost. Wireless security systems, including Ring and Simply Safe have made installation easy and cut customer costs for subscription and installation significantly. Additionally, these new systems can be self-monitored over long distances with a simple application, surpassing the capabilities of legacy systems. Communication software like Zoom have changed the way customers can conduct business or visit family and friends with a minimal subscription cost.

Referring back to the real estate market, online information has replaced the information power once held by real estate agents. Buyers can now get new listing information, accessible only by real estate agents in years past.

Virtually every commodity can be purchased online through a multitude of vendors.

Threat of New Entrants

Artificial intelligence (AI) and robotics are just two broad areas that will disrupt many of the business' sector's mode of delivery. Telemedicine in healthcare is changing delivery of patient care, as well as sensors that measure everything from blood pressure and heart rate to distance care while people remain in their homes. In a 2019 Forbes article, ten industries are identified as ripe for redefining customer access to services including real estate, insurance and financial markets.[44] More application software will arm consumers with direct access to data and commodities. Consider the plethora of industries that have become obsolete due to online access to data, such as travel, publishing, real estate, and brick and mortar retailers.

One of the key factors to measure when analyzing the threat of new entrants into the industry for which you are positioned is to assess the barriers to entry. Some examples of the barriers to enter the marketplace as a new business are: the cost of inventory, licensing and regulation, access to customers or reach, technological advances, patents and trademarks, existing customer loyalty and if your company is "first in market." This is not a complete list. Of course, the more profitable an industry becomes the greater likelihood of new entrants.

What increases the barriers to entry into an industry? Typically, a service company does not have the up-front costs of a manufacturing business. Auto manufacturing or the manufacturing of nuclear medical equipment are far more complex and cost intensive than manufacturing containers for Campbell soup. The higher the start-up costs the greater the barrier to entry. The food and healthcare industries are more regulated than book selling. The more regulated, the less likelihood of new entrants. Some businesses spend years obtaining patents or licensing before receiving a dollar of revenue, and companies that are the first to market typically have an edge against newcomers.

Competition Within the Industry

The force among competitors within a single industry is the greatest force. How diverse are the competitors, quality of goods and service, brand loyalty, the opportunity for growth in the industry, industry concentration, barriers to exit and switching costs among the competition? One way to measure the competition within an industry is to add the revenue of the top four competitors and divide by four. The resultant ratio will inform you if the industry is a monopoly, oligopoly or neither.

Food industry markets such as grocery chains and retail clothing stores are far more competitive than selling Middle Eastern bread or olives. The demand for a Rolls Royce is in a distinctive and exclusive market versus the SUV industry. The more lucrative the industry, you will see more entrants into it. Each competitor will make their move to become the head of the pack—to create a competitive advantage that will ensure the largest market share.

Analysis of Kate's Garden Using Porter's Model

From the beginning moments of drafting the architecture of my garden, every element that would compete with this plot of land, destined to be my safe haven, was considered. After all, despite owning the land, man is its greatest predator. The ground I carved out had been left to its natural "chaotic" state for the 20 years prior. Now I was going to disrupt a microsystem, colonizing this unkempt, weed infested, untamed underbrush with perimeters and somewhat alien plants. I was improving the space and hoped my good intentions would banish the bad.

The competition for land and its natural resources is centuries old. Countries around the world mark their history based upon their battles for and to preserve land. My garden is a microcosm of the earth's unremitting battle to protect and garner its natural resources. The competition is endless: weeds, rodents, deer, insects, disease and the environment itself. The sun, water and nutrients from the soil are endowing the roses as much as the weeds competing for the same. The fog in its moist blanket can envelop the leaves with a medium for fungus and black spot. Even the insects have a love-hate relationship with nature, as I have had a love-hate relationship with them. I'm in love with the beneficial bugs dining on the malicious ones that lay spores for the next generation to create chaos later—cutting, chewing and making dinner of the very leaves that give life to new buds.

As with business, the first year in operation can be an upward climb on the learning trajectory, yet, one of the most exhilarating; a sense that you and the business are learning together, to synchronize your next steps to maintain your gait—balancing and reinforcing toward a firm stride forward. In that first year of my expanded garden, 2007, most of my energy was being expended through my watchful eye, overseeing the blooming proliferation of plant life as the seeds uncovered their essence: germinating, sprouting and thrusting through the soil. I was almost giddy as I inspected what seemed a miraculous outcome. After months of planning, grading, prepping and overcoming one obstacle after another, I was ecstatic to finally see the birth of what had only been a dream. I was awestruck by the new life pushing through layers of soil. Oh, the wonderment of the shiny, deep green, blemish-free leaves unfolding, and the tiny buds erupting; each plant forced upright, frail but strengthening. It felt as if only the healthy parts of nature were aware of the garden and I was there simply to mix the right ingredients—tending to what nature had brought forth.

That first year I was spellbound by the beauty of this place of homage to my dad. I couldn't believe the lack of intrusions to what felt like my paradise. I became almost indolent toward needed work, as the garden seemed to maintain itself, giving me daily joy.

As the seasons turned the corner from spring to summer then autumn, I was exuberant with its outcome. My somnolence, however, lulled me into a fantasy—dreaming things would remain as abundant as in year one. In the spring of my second year, 2008, I would be stricken with a new appreciation for what nature accomplishes when one fails to anticipate change.

The winter laid down new seeds, blown from the winds, expelled by the birds and tracked under the earth by moles, gophers and ground squirrels. As if an army of invaders planned their attack for the spring solstice, a sudden intrusion of new, unwanted life, death and disruption unfolded. I was not only taken off guard but horrified at nature's forces against me and my vestibules and chambers of roses, dahlias, and arrays of floral beauty. Even spring's young growth was speckled with aphids, spider mites and larvae armed to spread and destroy. Fungus was clothing my rose leaves with rust and black spot, even ahead of the ensuing fog that claims each June and July. The worst was yet to come. The once vivid David Austin blooms were now severely weakened by their uprooted balls, teetering over and fighting for life. The invasion of weeds seemed to happen overnight, as if D-day was underway, and I had never anticipated such an assault. A business owner who does not ready themselves for ensuing competition will likely be among the estimated 50 percent who fail in the first five years.

That first year, I was quieted by, what seemed to me, only the good sides of nature being aware of my garden. The richness of its virgin soil, protected by wire and absence of pests and unwanted weeds, led me to thinking this Eden would only bring bliss. By year two, all the elements of nature that once inhabited this space returned to reclaim it.

After the gophers invaded the underbelly of my roses, in a single night, I sent out a distress signal to my garden crew. My first responders descended on my rose garden, extricated each rose bush and wrapped the rootball in wire before replanting. In time, without the attentive oversight of natural resources, the garden's sustainability is threatened. *In business, without being hypervigilant to anticipate ensuing risk, mitigating thereof, and/or failing to be proactive, sustainability is threatened.*

Reflect in Your Garden

Porter's Model of Five Forces is a strategic planning tool that needs to be utilized to keep a pulse on your external competition. Take a moment to analyze each one of the forces impacting your business. If you're contemplating starting a business, assess your place among the competition in terms of your start-up's profitability.

Bargaining power of buyers?

Bargaining power of suppliers?

Threat of new entrants and barriers to entry?

Threat of substitutes?

Competition in your industry?

SUMMER

CHAPTER 3

Genesis of Emergency Specialists Corporation (ESC)

The Life Cycle of a Business

EMERGENCY SPECIALIST CORPORATION AS A START-UP (THE SEED)

I was inspired to be a nurse after reading *A Cap for Kathy* by Kathy Martin,[45] at a young age. My aunts, Evonne and Violet, were first-generation immigrants who became nurses. My uncle, Robert Early, a Harvard-educated surgeon, became one of the first surgeons to specialize in pediatrics. My Uncle Eugene Nakfoor, a family practitioner who became an emergency medicine physician, would have a significant impact on my life and business pursuits.

I was a high school graduate in 1970, celebrating the last of 12 years of Catholic school education, looking for hospital experience to strengthen my application to nursing school. I was so discouraged after repeatedly being told *you need experience*, that I reached out to Uncle Eugene for any help he could offer. I finally garnered a part-time position as a clerk in the emergency department at St. Lawrence Hospital. The summer after graduation was to be the beginning of many eye-opening experiences working in an inner-city emergency department.

Summer Job in the ER

Rushed by ambulance
to the trauma room
doctors and nurses
move quickly

in unison
open your airway
cut off your clothes
assess the damage—

18-year-old male,
auto versus motorcycle—
that left you bludgeoned
bleeding and broken—
moaning

writhing to breathe
doctors shout orders
nurses attacked
every part of you
with life-saving measures

I witnessed my first trauma
shook with nerves
took order after order
requesting machines, medicines
and more experts—

consumed with tasks
I returned to my desk—
my role in this choreographed
effort of desperately keeping
you in our world

the next time I looked to the trauma room
down the long hall of exam rooms—
a clean, crisp, white sheet
covered the gurney where you had just laid

the stainless steel was shining again
floor waxed
room empty
staff gone—

back to performing
their abandoned tasks
as once before—

you awoke that day as I did
you had plans as I did
we were both 18

one moment you were
hinged to your motorcycle
then you lay in the morgue
a tag placed around your toe for the coroner
forty years ago now

perhaps we have traveled
together all the time
and maybe it was not your death
that changed my life—
but how quickly we turned to living after
you were gone

I was told by the nurses that history was being made in the emergency room at St. Lawrence Hospital. And, so it was. I listened to stories of how we were working with one of the first ever group of physicians to contract with a hospital to provide coverage in the emergency department 24 hours a day, seven days a week. I was working among the pioneers of this new specialty of emergency medicine being born right there in Lansing, Michigan (see "A Seed Carries Remnants").

Over the next three years of nursing school, I continued to work part-time in the ED. I was enamored with all the ED had to offer as a workplace of caring, learning and adventure. I attended class during the day, nursing clinical in the afternoon and work at night two to three nights a week. The ED was an escape from the rigors of studying; what an opportunity to lift the theory from books and apply it to the real world—a world most people never witness in a lifetime! Midway through nursing school, and educated to perform the tasks of a Licensed Vocational Nurse (LVN), doctors and nurses afforded me experiences in the clinical area that students rarely encountered. Often, I worked as both a clerk and LVN while getting paid only as a clerk, although the doctors thought I should be paid for both positions. I was young, eager and naïve.

Just prior to graduating from nursing school, my Uncle Eugene asked me into his office to inform me that he could not employ me as a registered nurse. He had been taunted about hiring his niece as a clerk and *wasn't going to be accused of nepotism*. Unexpectedly, a week later he reversed his decision under pressure from the nursing staff who petitioned him hard to hire me.

I retired my pink clerk uniform on Friday and went to work on Monday in white, proudly donning the cap and full black band as a graduate nurse. I was now senior to some of the staff who were my colleagues or superiors only days earlier. I had just celebrated my 21st birthday, and recall that summer as one of the most exciting times of my life.

Autumn was around the corner and I received the good news that I had passed my nursing boards and went from a graduate nurse to a registered nurse. Immediately, I was assigned to manage the entire night shift staff and the only RN for the eight hours between 11:00 p.m. and 7:00 a.m. Initially I was terrified going into work, wondering what trauma or emergency I would need to be prepared to manage alongside the physician. Arriving at my first night shift, assessing my patient in the trauma room—a victim of a motorcycle accident—I lifted saline dressings exposing the entire inside of his abdominal cavity.

I loved the challenge and anticipation of what was next. I was the only RN on the night shift and responsible for a high volume of critical patients (replaced by two RNs when I left). Without a doubt that first year of work as an emergency department charge nurse was life changing, however, despite those thrilling next two years, I began to yearn for something more challenging.

I began to ask myself, *Why couldn't nurses contract with the hospital to provide services as physicians do?* When I had the opportunity to dine with the founders of the American College of Emergency Physicians (ACEP) in Las Vegas, I again posed the question, *If physicians could subcontract with a hospital for specialty services, why not nurses? The physicians challenged me saying, You feel this way now, but you'll want a family and not want to be committed to a job.* I recall saying one word, *Bullshit!* It would be another five years before I could bring my idea of nurses subcontracting services to emergency departments to fruition.

I was 23 years old in August 1975 when I was recruited from St. Lawrence Hospital to Carmel Community Hospital's Emergency Department. I would work in tandem with the physician to manage the care of patients and staff on the night shift. However, after three years, and despite the idyllic setting of living in Carmel, California,

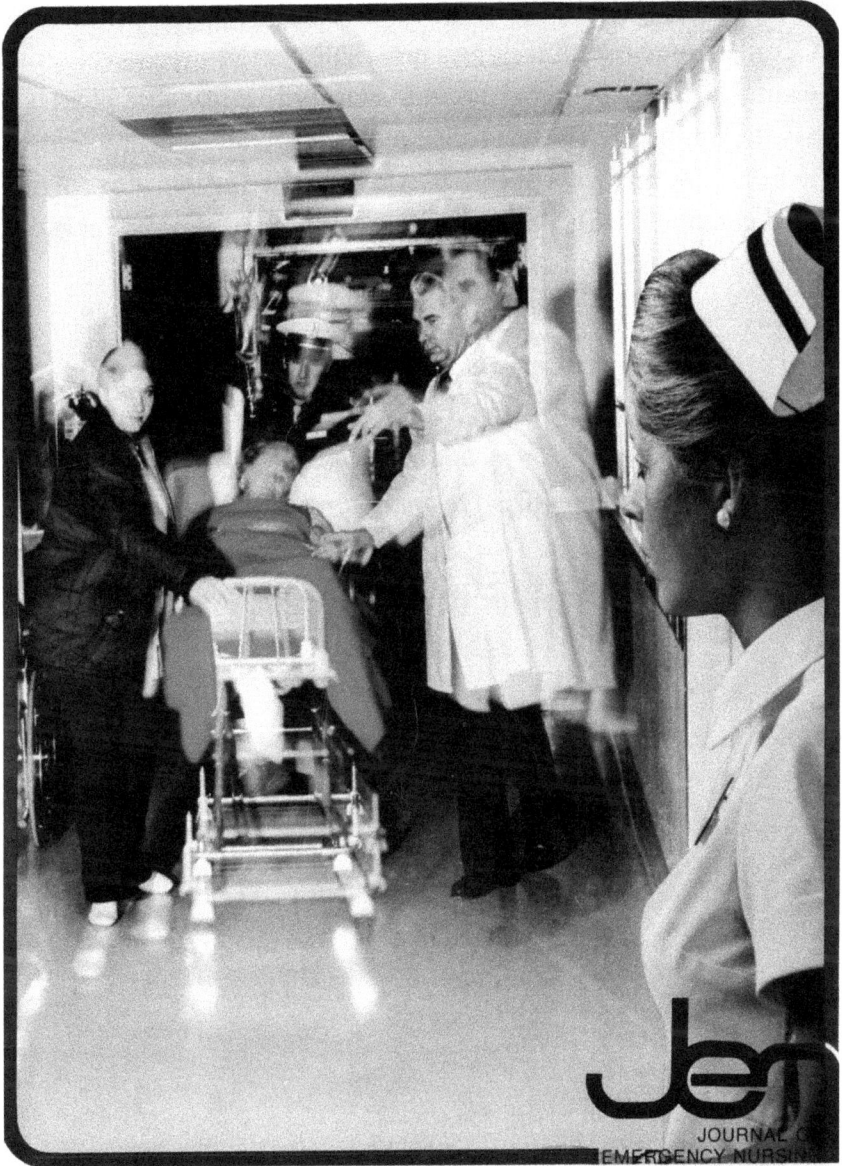

JER

JOURNAL OF EMERGENCY NURSING

OFFICIAL PUBLICATION OF THE EMERGENCY DEPARTMENT NURSES ASSOCIATION

Pictured above are Kate Nakfoor, RN (right) with Dr. John Wiegenstein, MD, at St. Lawrence Hospital. Dr. Wiegenstein was one of the eight founders of the American College of Emergency Medicine (ACEP), and ACEP's first President. Dr. Wiegenstein was instrumental in Emergency Medicine becoming a specialty.

paying $125 a month for a furnished cottage steps from the Pacific Ocean, I found myself seeking a new challenge. I moved to Palo Alto, California, after being accepted to Stanford University's physician assistant program. However, after much deliberation, I chose instead to finish pre-medical education. After completing two years of pre-med combined with a bachelor in nursing, I was now 28 years old, burned out on working and going to school full-time.

> *I asked, "If physicians could subcontract with a hospital for specialty services, why not nurses?" One of the ACEP founders said, "You'll feel this way now, but you'll want a family and not want to be committed to a job." I recall saying one word, "Bullshit!"*

A Seed Carries Remnants from the Past

Today, we assume paramedics will arrive prepared to care for us *in extremis*. We expect doctors and nurses specialized in emergency medicine and nursing when entering the emergency department. Yet, such a scene didn't exist prior to the mid-1960s when a convergence of forward thinking, risk-taking physicians stepped in to bridge this chasm.

In the mid 1960s a handful of physicians, mostly family practitioners in the Midwest, decided to contract with a hospital to cover the emergency room 24 hours a day, 7 days a week. Prior to this time you would find a nurse or bell to ring, summoning a nurse and/or doctor.

The entry of contracted physicians into the emergency department (ED) raised a series of previously unasked questions that quickly needed answers: how to bill for services, who was in charge of personnel and staffing, designing the flow of the department, how to be a trusted liaison to the patient's personal doctor, and what was the profile of doctor and nurse ready to treat all-comers seeking emergency care.

All these issues had to be addressed when Dr. Eugene Nakfoor became the first contracted Emergency Department Medical Director of St. Lawrence Hospital in Lansing, Michigan in the late 1960s. Doctor Nakfoor, John Wiegenstein, MD, and Gaius Clark, MD, were among the first to provide around-the-clock medical coverage for an inner-city emergency department. Dr. Nakfoor later became a resource for ED physicians after he developed a method of billing for professional services.

The ED nurses established, and the physicians implemented, the Scribe System placing a nurse as the pivot around whom the department flowed at maximum productivity.

The Scribe System's success was hinged on anticipatory, thorough preparation of the patient at every step so as to support the physician working effectively with the entire staff. In my 16 years employed in an emergency department, I would never work in one as efficient as St. Lawrence Hospital, due to the utilization of the Scribe System.

Additionally, Dr. Nakfoor negotiated an unprecedented concept called "departmental status." Departmental status gave him ultimate and final decision-making authority over the hiring of staff, accountability for performance of all personnel and flow of the department. Nurses traditionally were hired, staffed and held accountable to the Nursing Department, not so at St. Lawrence under the direction of Dr. Nakfoor. No nurses from outside the department were allowed to work in the emergency department and no ED nurses were allowed to work in other parts of the hospital. In 1967 this was novel (and remains more novel today). Not only were hospital-based physicians in non-teaching hospitals a rarity, but such authority over a hospital department was unprecedented.

Departmental status was a concept that was unheard of at that time and still arouses controversy today. When Dr. Nakfoor retired, the departmental status model was reversed and nurses once again reported to the Nursing Department; many of the other advances also ceased. Five years later I would draw upon the lessons learned from working with these pioneers in the field of emergency medicine and management.

If you want something new, you have to stop doing something old.

—Peter Drucker

Emergency Specialists Corporation—The Beginning

When a series of separate events or ways of thinking converge to influence large-scale change, such a confluence of events leads to innovations or shifts in thinking, also referred to as a tipping point, paradigm shift or timing. Such a convergence of events made way for Emergency Medicine to become the 23rd medical specialty in 1979.[46] That same year I determined the time was right for emergency department nurses to break down previously erected barriers and gain access into inaccessible areas.

A nationwide nursing shortage created the opportunity for companies providing temporary staffing to expand their businesses. However, hospitals were unable to staff the specialty areas of critical care, intensive care, operating room and emergency departments due to the dearth of qualified nurses and the resistance to allow "outsiders" into specialized areas. Some hospitals were forced to close these specialty areas or divert ambulance traffic to other hospitals due to this shortage of specialty nursing staff. My research showed no other companies were staffing emergency departments exclusively. While there were businesses providing critical care, intensive care and operating room nurses, the nurses were employees of such businesses. My dream was to subcontract emergency department nurses, just as ED physicians had done in years prior. As 1979 was underway, I was determined this was the opportune time to realize my goal of subcontracting emergency department nurses in Central California hospitals.

The county hospital where I worked was the area's poison center, a phone-in service for the public to access immediate answers to questions regarding overdoses or medications. As the night shift's nurse in charge, not only did I manage this inner-city emergency department staff (today a Level 3 trauma center), but gave orders to paramedics in the field as the mobile intensive care nurse (MICN) on duty, and was the advice nurse on the poison center line answering incoming calls. The county hospital was no different than surrounding hospitals, struggling to fully staff its specialty units. I recall, after being in charge of a shift that was short-staffed and performing the job of three people, I walked into the office of one of the ED manager's, a woman named Jenny, and said that the ED was an *accident waiting to happen*. It was the first of many conversations Jenny and I would have about resolving the ED staffing problem.

Jenny listened to what I planned to accomplish over the next year and that I was preparing to start a business subcontracting ED nurses. After several such conversations, she asked if I wanted a partner. She was willing to leave a secure, well-paying management position to join me in this uncertain, yet, *avant-garde* business venture. It would be close to a year before we could launch our endeavor, but verbally agreed that day to partner. The business name would be specific to emergency nurses, but not limiting us by specifying the services we would develop and market. We decided on Emergency Specialist Corporation (ESC) as our business identification. Despite spending unending hours to design ESC, I could only compare my excitement and exhilaration to that first year working in the ED nine years earlier.

ESC'S Organizational Development and Design

Neither Jenny nor I could afford to leave our jobs to devote the hours needed to construct our business. Due to the fact I worked night shift and Jenny day shift, I took on many of the tasks necessary to create the legal, tax and other elements of the operating side of our start-up. I also amassed a savings of $25,000 over several years working three jobs: moonlighting in other EDs, teaching firefighters and my full-time ED position at the county facility. I knew one day I would bring my business idea to fruition and worked hard to build a financial cushion in prior years. The $25,000 would be seed money for my future business and to support me for a short time until the business had net gains; however, *while busy planning my company, a nefarious stockbroker and his company, E.F. Hutton, stole every penny of my $25,000 placed in a savings account.* My lawsuit netted me $3,000, after all fees were paid and Hutton's admission of guilt for switching documents. Although I did learn terms like "margin" and "churning" from the experience; I also learned that I was as vulnerable as a kitten in coyote country.

I learned an indelible lesson to mistrust; however, I could trust myself to work hard and not let another person's pursuit of evil destroy my long-term vision.

Jenny and I had no formal business education at the time, but knew we could learn quickly. We needed an office but couldn't afford staff or much space. I found an executive office suite in a burgeoning business district of San Jose that provided reception and basic administrative services.

I researched corporate models and believed a subchapter-S was the best match. We were likely to have net losses in our first one to five years and could take these losses against our ordinary income. Through various referrals we found an accountant, Dennis, who was impressed with our idea and agreed to take us as clients, assisting with the independent contract model. I researched emergency department physician agreements, physician-to-physician and physician-to-hospital agreements as templates for ESC's independent contractor agreement. I hired an attorney, recommended by a physician contract group, to draft the contract between the hospitals and ESC and a separate subcontract between nurses and ESC. Jenny and I had a loosely established partnership agreement, again borrowing from templates finalized by our attorney. I tried to save money by doing some of the legwork myself, such as going directly to San Francisco to file corporate documents.

I created a marketing portfolio with which to approach over 30 hospital emergency department nurse managers and administrative staff; proceeding to meet managers from the San Francisco Bay area south 150 miles through the burgeoning tech industrial area of San Jose to agricultural communities of Gilroy, California. This was both an opportunity—a gap in the marketplace we were trying to fill—and a threat to the established practice of employing nurses.

Marketing to Hospitals and Building a Corps of Independent Contract Nurses

The ESC core business was modeled after temporary nurse staffing agencies, or registries. Our competitive advantage was specializing in emergency nurses and as an independent contractor versus the usual employee-employer relationship between the nurses and ESC. While there was a high demand for emergency room nurses, and no competition, we still had to convince ED managers and hospital administrators to utilize outside ED nursing staff—a concept unheard of at the time.

We confronted uncharted territory full of questions to be answered, just as emergency physicians faced a decade earlier. I set up a system of billing and chart of accounts, learning quickly the business of "operating a business" that was based on the never-before-idea of independently contracted emergency nurses. I was creating the template for operating this business model. However, the issue that kept me up at night was *how would we meet the demands of the hospitals with the availability of best-in-class nurses?*

In the beginning it wasn't easy to sell our idea. The emergency department nurse managers all greeted us with the same defensive argument—*no ED nurse can come from the outside and function in our department.* Nevertheless, our background working in inner-city, high-volume emergency departments made us a credible source. With confidence, we suggested they "just try us once."

Hospital administrators embraced the idea of independently contracted nurses, they were relieved of the headache of staffing and managing nurses. However, as the concept was catching on, barriers to entry were erected. While administrators were intrigued by the next step of taking over nurse staffing of the entire department, our greatest opponents were nurses and the hospitals' nursing departments. The resounding rebuff: *If ED nurses were allowed to be independent contractors, why not extend the opportunity to all critical care, intensive care and operating room nurses? What made ED nurses special?* Nursing departments were threatened and continued to express their resistance.

While Jenny and I were methodically contacting emergency departments throughout the Bay Area and Central Coast, we also undertook recruiting the highest caliber of emergency department nurses.

I benchmarked the fees charged for nurse services against the prevailing *per diem*, short-term, staff pay. ESC's competitive advantage was the subcontracting model. Emergency Department nurses were to become independent of the employer model and consider their skills as marketable. An important variable in ESC's cost of doing business was the decision to subcontract services with the nurses. No withholding taxes were taken out of the subcontracted nurses' paycheck, an amount close to 20 percent. ESC nurses were responsible for self-reporting their income and we provided the 1099 tax information. ESC nurses were excited about the opportunity to choose where and when to work in exchange for benefits and would rise to the occasion of being responsible for reporting such income as an independent contractor.

We did little advertising for nurses and had no trouble attracting them based on our reputation, and the nurses were motivated to be independent. We had a plethora of nurses who had approached us for work; each wanted to know when they could start and expressed interest in shifts wherever we had contracts. Jenny and I had numerous contacts in the world of emergency nursing and many of the first to apply were our colleagues and leaders in high volume, inner-city, emergency departments. I never tired of promoting or explaining our goals and mission of ED nurses' independence.

We were attracting nurses with a range of goals: putting kids through college, looking for extra shifts for various monetary reasons, working full-time for us, and just being part of a groundbreaking idea for the future of nurses. We held weekly information meetings with our accountant, Dennis, as guest speaker. He outlined the concept and responsibilities of being an independent contractor versus an employee. Each week we filled the room with interested nurses ready to sign up for shifts.

Only the top-performing, experienced emergency department nurses were considered as candidates for ESC. I created both a written and oral exam as part of the hiring process. Frankly, any nurse who self-selected to work for ESC was of a caliber unafraid of change, extremely adaptable and of an unconventional spirit. We attracted seasoned emergency department nurses who could walk into any emergency department, of any size or location, and take on the most critical of patients. She/he would meld nicely into the flow of the emergency department, and, just as the independent contractor model aspired, arrive to the ED with the skill set necessary to perform at a high level.

Balancing Demands

To meet the demands of the hospitals with the availability of best-in-class nurses, we needed to make sure there was enough work for the nurses and enough nurses for the work—comparable to homeostasis in nature. However, meeting the demand for nurses was not always achieved for a variety of reasons, especially due to the short notice we were often given for the high-caliber ED nurses with whom we contracted.

> *Frankly, any nurse who self-selected to work for ESC was of a caliber unafraid of change, extremely adaptable and of an unconventional spirit. We attracted seasoned emergency department nurses who could walk into any emergency department, of any size or location, and take on the most critical patients.*

In the early years of ESC we heard a lot of defensiveness from ED charge nurses. They told us time and again that they had never used people from the outside and were not going to start anytime soon. However, breakthroughs came when ED managers and charge nurses needed a full complement of nurses they couldn't fill with regular staff, with the highest demand for weekends and night shifts. Our strategy was one of action by providing only quality nurses and demonstrating that this new paradigm had merit.

GROWTH PHASE OF **ESC**

During the growth phase of a business, the organization is now determining if it will continue to expand and establish new markets, sell to a larger company that can take it to its next step, or bring in new leadership to move the company forward. At this stage, an organization may expand by entering new markets, by diversifying or can simply remain status quo as a small, surviving business.

An idea doesn't have to be revolutionary, but could in fact be a slight change in the way we look at something. For small businesses incremental change may make more sense, as the danger of expanding too quickly—overextending money and resources— can be real and sometimes ruinous.

Within the first year, Emergency Services Corporation garnered nine emergency department contracts and revised its fees to better compensate the nurses. I conducted a gap analysis, investigating where we should position ESC in the marketplace for the future, and realized we needed to expand our model to include intensive care and critical care nurses as independent contractors. Our volume doubled as a result of this decision.

Where's Your Business Plan?

In the growth phase, customers are learning about the business and creditors may be willing to give money as the company expands. ESC was evolving so quickly we were having difficulty paying our nurses until we could collect on our accounts receivables. We decided it was time to ask for a bank loan. We were young and didn't know what we didn't know; after all, why shouldn't a bank loan us money? We were two hardworking nurses with a small business that served a unique purpose, and had every intention of paying back the loan. Boy was I naive. Our accountant made an appointment with the vice president of his bank.

We were greeted by a kind-looking gentleman who explained he was meeting with us at the behest of Dennis, our accountant. Little did we know this banker was accustomed to meeting with multimillion-dollar venture capitalists. Frankly, we were quite sure our business ranked among the top entrepreneurial ventures of its time. We were oblivious to the fact we were entering the bank with crumbs as collateral for gold. Our business idea was a tip at the local diner to this bank manager; however, he was attentive and deliberate. After explaining our business concept to him, assuring him we just needed a loan to cover our payroll and would pay it back quickly, he looked down at his desk then slowly upward at me and asked, "Where is your business plan?" Jenny and I looked at each other in wonderment. We had no idea what a business plan was, let alone provide one. Upon explaining our failure to come prepared with such a document, he looked up at us incredulously, "You come to me asking for a loan and you have no business plan?" Without adequately understanding his astonishment at our request, our sense was we lacked something substantial—the key that would unlock our loan. He was considerate to suggest the Small Business Administration.

Deflated, we did follow up with a request for a loan with the Small Business Administration (SBA). We were under the impression this organization existed to help individuals like us who simply needed short-term capital to cover expenses. I understand the need for collateral, however, being women with a new business concept that was in the early stages of operation, we were considered a high risk. Had I not lost the seed money, we wouldn't have needed a loan. Oddly, because we were so successful, we did need money to make payroll. Why should we have to own a home or another small business to place at risk for this minor loan? I couldn't understand why we would be asked to place something worth ten times what we were asking to borrow as collateral. I figured that if we had so much to offer as risk, why would we be asking for money? We left the SBA office both angry and frustrated. We decided to privately finance our business and sought the help of individual, private investors. My boyfriend and I each put several thousand dollars of our savings into the business to cover payroll. We never would have made payroll without the infusion of capital from the two of us. (See the Anita Roddick vignette in Chapter 6 on leadership.)

Don't Float My Check!

I invoiced ESC's hospital clients each week. Two of our contract hospitals were notorious for failing to pay us within the 30-day contractual agreement. After multiple calls to the financial department, accounts payable (AP), I finally walked into the AP departments of these two hospitals, unannounced, requesting a face-to-face meeting with our business contact. On both occasions I stood across the desk from the male representative and explained we were a small business operating on a tiny margin, and not one of the many large suppliers whose checks he was used to floating. The accounts payable representative opened his desk drawer, and, behold, our checks were face-up waiting for me to receive them.

Before your product hits the market, you need to reinvent it.

—Peter Drucker

I conducted a gap analysis, investigating where we should position ESC in the marketplace for the future, and realized we needed to expand our model to include intensive care and critical care nurses as independent contractors

---

ESTABLISHMENT

Connecting the Dots

Steve Jobs, in his memorable 2001 commencement speech at Stanford University, spoke about "connecting the dots." He described experiences throughout his life that later contributed to the development of much bigger things. For example, his exposure to a course in calligraphy led to his implementation of multiple fonts in Apple's application software. I, too, share a few "connect-the-dots" experience that propelled ESC into new markets.

In addition to working in an emergency department for many years while I was in my twenties, I sought more in-depth education and challenges in my field. Nationally I was among the first to sit for the emergency nursing certification exam. A second opportunity I seized was getting certified to teach in a junior college. My first assignment was to prepare 160 firefighters to qualify for the Emergency Medical Technician (EMT) exam (a bit daunting at 26 years old). Ironically, the day after lecturing on birthing a baby, the two heroic firefighters and I appeared on the front page of the local paper congratulating the skilled firefighters on their successful delivery of a baby into the local community. This was in the late 70s during the birth of Silicon Valley. For all I know the EMTs may have delivered a start-up CEO.

A third accomplishment that would later play a role in ESC's business development, was to be among the first ED nurses across the country to take on the added responsibility as a mobile intensive care nurse (MICN). Through a program at Stanford Medical Center, ED nurses were educated to gives orders to paramedics in the field via the emergency department's "base station"—a task only ED physicians previously performed.

Leveraging the MICN, I was in a position to propel ESC into unchartered territory. ESC provided the first nurse-assisted transport in the Santa Clara County area.

In 1986, a few years after launching ESC, the federal government passed the Emergency Medical Treatment and Labor Act (EMTALA) which made it a federal crime to transfer a patient *in extremis* to another hospital. As emergency department nurses working in a hospital considered a "safety net" hospital (the county facility open to all-comers), Jenny and I were aware of this rapidly increasing problem. The county hospital, where we worked prior to launching ESC, became the locus of "patient dumping," a last resort accepting all patients. We knew other local hospitals would welcome the opportunity to accept patients knowing they could be safely transferred to the county hospital, or hospitals able to accept patients, if they could be transferred by ambulance assisted by a nurse in transit. So Jenny and I approached the Emergency Medical System's (EMS) director with the idea of utilizing ESC nurses for such inter-hospital transfers.

My first political deal-making encounter was eye-opening and unforgettable. Jenny and I met with the EMS director who sat attentively while we laid out our idea. The director nodded affirmatively and promised to back our plan when it came time for all the stakeholders to vote on whether or not to take our proposal forward with a contract. However, when we arrived for the stakeholder's hearing, the director moved his chair so we were to his back and he all but ignored us. Nonetheless, his positional power base (see Bases of Power) was not going to deter us. We fought strategically and with sheer tenacity eventually won the contract.

ESC expanded into offering courses in advanced cardiac life support (ACLS) to hospitals. Many licensed staff had to renew their ACLS certification as a condition of work. The certification renewal was frequent and there was always demand for such courses. Finally, with Jenny's contacts, we branched into medical review of legal cases and served as experts for attorneys in emergency nursing-related litigations.

Although nurse-assisted transports, teaching certifying courses and providing medical-legal expertise were not sustainable businesses separately, adding approximately fifteen percent of our gross income, however, the more we could offer hospitals and the community, the more we solidified our position as the experts in emergency department nursing. With these forward-thinking decisions ESC stayed ahead of the S Curve.

Reflect in Your Garden

While ESC was a start-up business with rudimentary practices, some of the issues that arose creating ESC are similar to any business.

Have you created a business plan for your start-up idea?

Have you created a strategic plan? If so, has it been updated this year?

Are you prepared with a line of credit or have enough retained earnings in the event of a change in cash flow?

What is the rate of turnover in your accounts receivable?

FALL

CHAPTER 4

Maturity and Decline

C haracteristics of a mature business are steady growth with a more efficiently run operation to overcome the relatively lower growth rate. A mature business typically has amassed a cushion of retained earnings, or savings, that is reinvested or distributed to shareholders in the form of dividends. Maturity brings with it the foresight to see possible growth into a new business. Other features of a business reaching maturity is an established customer base and predictable product lines, Coca Cola and McDonald's are such businesses. However, this position has limited sustainability without innovations, strategically performing postmortems on products, replacing older ideas and products with new ideas and a refreshed customer base.

ESC saw a rapid trajectory upward with brisk growth and development into diversification. Just as Jenny and I were securing further growth, procuring more hospital contracts, our journey into maturity was far afield.

CONVERGENCE OF NEGATIVE FORCES: THE IRS, NURSES STRIKES AND DEATH

Entering our third year in business, as we were negotiating our biggest contracts to date, the perfect storm was on the horizon. We were about to face unprecedented events and unexpected threats that would test our ability to weather the squall.

The Internal Revenue Service (IRS)

The medical center, where Jenny and I worked prior to launching our business, was classified as a tertiary teaching facility. A tertiary center received the most severe cases of trauma, and patients needing specialized care. One or two medical complexes of its type served millions in a metropolitan area. Such facilities were staffed 24 hours a day, seven days a week, with specialists and equipment only found in a teaching medical center of its class. Stanford Medical Center and the University of San Francisco are two such complexes in the area.

Jenny and I had contracts with medical facilities, classified today as a Level 1 or 2 trauma center, but this hospital was a Level 3 facility. Not only would we contract for ED nursing services but also provide nurses to the multiple critical care areas. While we were also in negotiations with four other facilities, securing this contract would be our largest, most profitable and prestigious to date. As a result of our history with the hospital and sound business reputation we felt confident in consummating the deal.

Sitting down for what we believed to be the final negotiating session, the administrator prefaced his opening remarks with, *I would not ordinarily share this information, but because of your service to our organization*...he then presented us with a letter meant only for the eyes of administration from the California Hospital Council. The letter informed administration to *beware of contracting with nurses holding themselves out to be independent contractors.* While no precedent case existed, the letter implied that hospitals could be at risk for tax obligations as a result of utilizing our services. This letter posed an ominous threat for the future of ESC. Let me explain the underlying issues.

Under the rulings of the IRS, to qualify as an "independent contractor" several criteria must be met: supply your equipment, be responsible for your schedule, supervise yourself, be the contracting entity, be responsible for all benefits, including health insurance, pay for travel expenses and continuing education. The independent contractor may deduct work-related expenses against income.

ESC would pay an additional 18 percent plus the contracted rate for an employee should we withhold taxes. Today, this expense is upwards of 35 percent. An employer pays half of social security withholding, but the independent contractor pays the entire amount. Despite the issuance of 1099 declarations to our independent contractors, the IRS assumed the contractor would not pay their entire amount due.

ESC was not without its own risk from the IRS, however, the hospitals not only had deeper pockets but were giving direction and providing resources to the nurses while at work. Such direction created a gray area when meeting the independent contractor status; putting the hospitals at greater danger of being classified as an employer.[47]

The California Hospital Council's letter warned hospitals that should they utilize independently contracted nurses, as was the case of ESC, and, in the event the independent nurses failed to pay their withholding tax, the IRS could hold the hospital liable for the unpaid taxes as the *employing entity*. The risk of utilizing ESC's subcontracted nurses appeared to outweigh their benefit, and the threat was an unwanted liability.

Jenny and I decided to request an *off the record* IRS review of ESC to seek their opinion as to whether our nurses met the criteria to justify the independent contractor status. The ability to independently contract for nursing services was not only one of our competitive advantages, but the foundation of our ideals and core values, upon which the business was built.

(Note: To put our dilemma into context, it would be 40 years later, an extensive legal and legislative battle at both the federal and state levels and more than a quarter of a billion dollars spent to fight this very issue by other companies, such as Uber, attempting to advance independent contracting as a business model. (See text box Independent Constractors 2021.)

Four Hospital Strikes: Nurses and Living Your Code of Ethics

Anticipating the surge in business as a result of the contracts we were negotiating, Jenny and I accelerated our campaign to subcontract more nurses in a variety of critical care specialties. Nurses working with us began to inform us of rumors of an unprecedented nurses' strike: four hospitals in a fifteen-mile radius were planning to strike simultaneously! Among the hospitals were tertiary medical centers serving not only a regional population, but prominent in the international community for their premiere research. Combined, their impact on the population within a metropolitan area was significant. Such a strike had bittersweet consequences for us and the stability of ESC. The rumor of strike became reality when I received a call from three of the striking hospitals asking if a contract for services could be negotiated, as they looked forward to utilizing our nurses. Not one of the four hospitals had been willing to contract with us over the past two years, yet, suddenly without any due diligence, we were invited to forward our contract to administration for signing.

If some of you reading this find the idea of an administration unilaterally signing a service contract without months of review implausible, let me remind you the model of our delivery system was far simpler than today. At the time, hospitals were freestanding and not horizontally and vertically integrated within a consortium of like-kind facilities as exists in complex organizations today.

Many of ESC subcontracted nurses worked full-time for one of these four striking hospitals. While not affiliated with one hospital, we were nurses first, representing an *esprit de corps* of nurses who looked to Jenny and me as leaders in the nursing community.

Companies should have a mission statement representing their core values or code of ethics. A placard on the wall means nothing until its meaning is challenged; individually, our core values are meant to guide us when tested as to what lines we will or will not cross. If our personal core values do not align with our workplace, internal conflict will arise and a choice of what overrules eventually occurs.

As an entrepreneur, consider this scenario: You're given an opportunity to financially secure your company, however, the clients with whom you contract represent a separation from your core values. Would you consummate the contract?

> *The core values of a business must be a living representation of the true guiding principles of the company; the "will-not-compromise" aspects of the company cannot be thrown away on a whim, but rather are steadfast pillars.*

We decided *not* to enter into a contract with any of the striking hospitals—despite the opportunity for extraordinary monetary gain. Did this cost us the financial solvency of the business? Should we have put the business above our personal and professional core values? As a business owner, one must determine the line they will not cross no matter the financial advantages to their company. The core values of a business must be a living representation of the true guiding principles of the company; the "will-not-compromise" aspects of the company cannot be thrown away on a whim, but rather are steadfast pillars.

Reflect in Your Garden

As an entrepreneur, consider this scenario: Your company needs a cash infusion to remain solvent during an unusually difficult period (i.e., COVID-19) and is unable to secure a loan. You're given an opportunity to financially secure your company with a new contract; however, the clients with whom you contract represent a separation from your core values. Would you consummate the contract?

How did you respond when running a business, working for an organization or in a relationship when you were challenged with an ethical dilemma? Would you make the same choices today?

Examine the core values of your company. Do these ideals represent the real values you espouse and that will direct you when faced with an ethical conflict?

❧

Death

Jenny called me to deliver the news that her husband had died suddenly and unexpectedly, the consequence of a heart anomaly in his early 40s. Little time passed before Jenny reevaluated her commitment to the business; her financial status changed, as well as her dedication to ESC. The fallout of this tragedy destabilized an already shaky structure.

ESC had an established customer base but we needed more contracts to be sustainable. Without additional contracts we were facing decline. While we did finalize two contracts at smaller hospitals, one of which utilized our nurses to staff their rural hospital emergency department, the hospitals with whom we held contracts reduced their usage more than fifty percent as a result of the California Hospital Council's letter.

The IRS informed us that "nurses could not be independent contractors," as they were under the supervision of others. We did not have the resources to fight a protracted battle with the IRS (see Uber vs. California Supreme Court below). The choice to not cross picket lines would prove costly. As the roller coaster headed downhill, one more car was occupied by Jenny who had become emotionally and physically absent.

The amassing of the perfect storm seemed to seal the fate of ESC: the IRS ruling, a four-hospital nursing strike that forced Jenny and me to confront our choices based upon our core values, the unexpected death of a business partner's husband, and her subsequent withdrawal emotionally and physically from the business, culminated in the demise of ESC.

After a short period of grief, I came to the decision that I wanted to salvage what remained of the business. I wanted to keep the name and potentially resurrect ESC under a different model, without sacrificing the independent contract idea. However, Jenny wanted to be bought out—a request I couldn't afford to fulfill.

The culmination of events resulted in the death of ESC. I was devastated! I was also too young and lacked the experience to strategize an alternate plan to save the business.

The Obituary

ESC's obituary read: *Two bright, ambitious, entrepreneurial individuals and their innovative idea was put to rest. The owners were caught in a storm of unexpected events; disease of unknown etiology took the life of a long-term dream of Ms. Nakfoor...culminating in an ending, all too soon and sudden.*

Sympathy went out to all those concerned: the 80-plus nurses, 13 hospitals, administrators and the many patients who may have benefited from the innovative ideas of two, young, less-than-prepared nurses who were ahead of their time.

Once it was clear the business had no future, the beginning of the final details of putting ESC to rest began. Jenny withdrew by failing to show up for work. I was to figure out the details of dissolution. Just as in marriage, entering into the contract is much easier than exiting, as was the untangling of ESC. I would be left to handle the legal, accounting, financial and tax dissolution documentation.

I informed nurses, hospitals and all parties related to ESC's business operation. Hospitals and nurses were notified in writing and given direction as to tax reporting; 1099s were issued and corporate dissolution papers completed.

ESC Was Ahead of Its Time

The dissolution of ESC represented more than the closing of a business but the end of a dream of mine. I had a vision of shifting the way nurses thought of themselves: from an employee to an independent contractor with a license and marketable skill set. The choice and opportunity for nurses to practice independently also concluded.

My vision proved to be years ahead of its time. Without the blessing of the IRS, ESC was doomed. I could have been sole shareholder, and the nurses strike would not change our mission and success over the long-term, but without my willingness to move to an employee-employer relationship, ESC had no future. I could not afford a battle with the IRS over the gray areas of nurses qualifying as independent contractors, and had no one in my camp to fight the battle with me. This was a painful time for me, much like saying goodbye to a loved one, or ending a relationship that held hopes for a future.

What next?

Just as there are cycles in nature— growth, senescence, death— I, too, had to regroup, going inward to assimilate and understand the three years I spent leading ESC. After the company was dissolved, I decided to embark on a new adventure—opening like a hesitant flower—this time in sales and marketing for a technology company in the Bay Area. This was something completely different than what I had previously undertaken. At my new job, I won the largest hospital information system contract in northern California and received salesperson of the year award. I grieved the loss of my business, and prepared myself for my next independent venture, returning to school to earn a graduate degree in business administration.

My Garden is Vast

My garden is vast
the many holes
dug by me

each fragment
of soil shoveled—
a piece of me

I have tripped
fallen into my failures—
and survived

Independent Contractors in 2021: Uber vs. California Supreme Court—The Voters Decide

The case for independent contractors: the qualifying provision that continues to be challenged in the courts is whether the contracting agency has "control" over the independent contractor. An April 12, 2018 Reuters article informs us a U.S. District Court Judge in Philadelphia ruled: Uber limousine drivers are not employees based upon the conclusion that the drivers are not under enough "control" to be considered employees.[48] This was definitely a "win" for Uber. Yet, the decision as to who is responsible for paying withholding taxes and workers' compensation was also decided in the California Supreme Court case *Dynamex vs. Los Angeles Superior Court*, State of California: "Workers whose roles are clearly comparable to those of employees include individuals whose services are provided within the usual course of the business of the entity for which the work is perform[ed]."[49] Also, in July 2018, the Dynamax case added teeth to what had been the criteria for determining employee versus independent contractor status since the Borello and Sons 1989 case.[50]

In a September 7, 2020 article in *The Law Review*, "Court Rules that Uber and Lyft Cannot Treat California Drivers as Independent Contractors," states that the Superior Court of California ruled Uber and Lyft drivers are to be treated as employees versus independent contractors, using the Dynamex Operations case as precedent to this decision. People of the State of California v. Uber Technologies is targeting the gig economy—disallowing Uber and Lyft drivers to be classified as independent contractors practicing in California. This has repercussions for both employer (Uber) and employee (drivers). Should Uber be classified as an employer, the most significant impact is their requirement to pay an additional 35 to 45 percent, above the base salary, to the employee, or driver, for benefits. Additionally, Uber will be responsible for scheduling and direction to employees, and likely play more of a role in the equipment Uber drivers utilize.

The drivers will no longer be able to decide when and where they choose to work, and no longer receive income as a 1099 employee. In turn, drivers will not be responsible for the entire portion of social security, as the employer will pay half of this withholding as part of the benefit package. Employees are not able to file a schedule C on their tax return and deduct any expenses incurred as an independent contractor. Due to the controversy over this issue, a proposition was placed on California's November 2020 ballot. The voters decided in favor of Uber and other gig economy drivers to work as independent contractors.

The combined contribution of the biggies in the gig economy: Uber, Lyft, DoorDash and Liftcart, ***exceeded $200 million dollars*** to successfully overturn the California Superior Court's decision and win the majority vote of California's Proposition 22 allowing app drivers to be classed as independent contractors for tax purposes.[51]

Despite the Uber, et al's win in November, the battle continues. In February 2021, app drivers requested the California Supreme Court to overturn the vote of California voters, however, the higher court rejected the request.[52] Will the battle never end?

The take-away after all these years is that my dream, my vision of giving nurses the choice to practice independently, was ahead of its time and a battle we could not have won.

WHY BIG BUSINESS FAILS: LESSONS LEARNED

Some plants have the capacity to live on for thousands of years: The Quaking Aspen tree (*Populus tremuloides*), has cloned itself for 80,000 years, and, while declining in numbers, remains in Utah as a single grove that has the appearance of multiple single trees. The Jurupa Oak, found in Crestmore Heights, California, the *Quercus palmeri*, is 13,000 years old. Noted in his book, *The Hidden Life of Trees*, Peter Wahlleben discusses the importance of "roots" as the source of history that holds the answers for the longevity of the 9500-year-old Norwegian Spruce, discovered by Leif Kullman.[53] The giant sequoias can live 3,200 years and redwoods an average of 1,500 years.[54]

While trees are the honored tribesman with ancient histories, as Herman Hesse tells us, some businesses do appear to display amazing longevity. Here's a list of some you may recognize, with the year they began: Jim Beam (1795), Pabst Brewing Company (1844), JP Morgan Chase (1799), Citigroup (1812), DuPont (1802), Colgate (1806), Dixon Ticonderoga (1795), HarperCollins (1817), Brooks Brothers (1818), and Macy's (1843).[55]

So what separates these companies from a plethora of large and small organizations that fail? Greed? Hubris? Short-sightedness? We know the obvious reasons but what leads individuals to want to take such risk, hold such power and potentially destroy so many people's lives as a result?

Approaching this problem in the spirit of learning, we can surmise that sometimes the fault lies with those in charge: witness the mismanagement of the TWA airline innovator, Howard Hughes, an eccentric owner who made erratic decisions that certainly affected the bottom line of his organization.

Trees are sanctuaries. Whoever knows how to speak to them, whoever knows how to listen to them, can learn the truth. They do not preach learning and precepts, they preach, undeterred by particulars, the ancient law of life.[56]

Hermann Hesse, *Bäume, Betrachtungen und Gedichte*

When we are stricken and cannot bear our lives any longer, then a tree has something to say to us: Be still! Be still! Look at me! Life is not easy, life is not difficult. Those are childish thoughts... Home is neither here nor there. Home is within you, or home is nowhere at all.

Hermann Hesse, *Bäume, Betrachtungen und Gedichte*

Excerpts from *"Wandering"*

Despite dominating the East Coast in commercial flights and becoming among the top four carriers nationally, Eastern Airlines headed into a downward spiral and the largest bankruptcy prior to 1991 due to the 1978 Air Deregulation Act and new competition.

How does the biggest international air carrier in the world, circa 1927 to 1991, Pan American Airlines, fall from its prestigious position? Notwithstanding its reputation for innovation, the rise in fuel prices and less demand during the Gulf War were contributors to its final landing in 1991. However, the bomb explosion over Lockerbie, Scotland, that killed all 259 passengers is considered the most significant cause of its demise.

Then there are companies so big that greed and dishonesty become the *modus operandi*—companies like Enron whose name is equated with corporate corruption and fraud. Enron's stock freefall from $91.00 to $0.67 a share in two years after a posted earnings of $111 billion in 2000 is a case study in avarice, fraud and corruption that displaced 22,000 workers. Or consider Lehman Brothers, whose involvement in the subprime mortgage crisis, negligence and excessive risk-taking, signaled the beginning of the Great Recession (2008) and collapse of the housing market. WorldCom was the big daddy of sleaze, hiding debt and overestimating assets, landing its CEO in prison for 25 years.

Then there are those who just don't keep up with the times, read the signs, continuously scan the competition, and are therefore unable to stay ahead of the S–curve. The Eastman Kodak Company's failure to see the future of digital photography, despite being the pioneer in this technology, is the best illustration of such oversight. In fact, in 1975, Kodak's digital camera release was the first of its kind. Similarly, Blockbuster video rental stores eventually embraced the innovation of streaming services, however, the CEO John Antioco, who was behind this vision, was fired and streaming services scaled back—an enormous mistake for the organization.

Compaq computers held the edge in the personal computer (PC) market after redesigning the IBM PC, introduced in 1982. Unfortunately, in the late 1990s, a merger with DEC (considered a travesty), growing competition by Dell and billions invested in a poorly designed chip, led to its downfall. Even Hewlett Packard's acquisition couldn't prevent it from a slow death in 2013.

> *The causes usually cited for failure of a company are costs of start-up, overruns on costs, depreciation of excess inventory, competition—anything but the actual cause, pure and simple bad management.*[57]
>
> —W. Edwards Deming

Occasionally, and for reasons not unlike those of Kodak's failure to foresee the market for one of its inventions, an otherwise breakthrough product was basically given away. This is the case of Bell Labs 1950s sale of one of its earliest transistor patents to the Tokyo Telecommunications System (TTS), later called Sony. AT&T, owner of Bell Labs, signed an agreement with the Justice Department to share its innovations as a means to avoid AT&T's break-up.[58] For a $25,000 patent-licensing fee, Bell Labs shared its technology with 40 paying companies at its Transistor Technology Symposium. Shortly after, TTS released its transistor clock, hearing aids and transistor radio prototype.[59] Fortunately for AT&T, there were many more innovations in the pipeline, like the first laser and satellite, leading to at least nine Nobel awards. Today Bell Labs is owned by Nokia.

Sometimes businesses simply fall prey to trends/tendencies/fashion innovations and oligopolies. Witness sadly the collapse of bookstores all across the United States, and even such mega-giants as Borders and Barnes & Noble (still in business as of this writing, but strug-gling).[60] The soon-to-be extinct paper publications, landlines, and cable companies are all also falling prey to new technologies. Some musicians feel cheated in the newer user-centric remuneration system that companies such as Spodify and Apple use versus the traditional payment system; similar changes apply to fine artists using mediums like Shutterstock to market their photos.[61]

Reflect in Your Garden

*Take a nice long walk among the trees and listen for the answers.
I do believe nature teaches us much if we just rest quietly and
meditate on what you want to learn.*

*Do you look for answers in all the obvious places or delve deep
and into the roots of an issue?*

Allow yourself the silence to hear the answers.

*Is your company threatened by emerging competition and how
are you strategically planning for change?*

What are the "roots" of your business' success or struggle?

WINTER

You can't manage what you don't measure.

—W. Edward Deming

What gets measured gets improved.

—Peter Drucker

PART II

The Boring But Important Stuff

Most theories discussed in this book are conceived from mathematical computations and scientific applications that have been adapted by other disciplines, including business. The most applicable is Systems Theory—a combination of Computer Theory, the Second Law of Thermodynamics (entropy), and Cybernetics, and draws on the 1945 and 1948 work of Ludwig von Bertalanffy's General Systems Theory.[62] Later in the chapter, I will also include Complexity Science, a more recent dimension to Systems Theory that expands upon von Bertalanffy's original ideas.

CHAPTER 5

Systems Theory

To appreciate the interconnectedness of nature and business—in fact, all elements of life—we'll look at the concept of systems theory and, subsequently, systems thinking. Ludwig von Bertalanffy described General Systems Theory originally in 1947 and in his 1964 book of the same name. He said that *Infinite examples of a system exist—from the single cell, a micro system, to the universe, a macro system.*[63]

Among the many theories I have studied and taught, systems theory is the most relevant when understanding the interrelationships of parts relative to the whole, and why I believe we cannot solve a problem in one area without understanding the connection of each system to the whole.

A complex system with which we are all familiar is the human body. Our body is composed of many micro, or smaller, systems within a greater, or macro, organization consisting of: circulatory, respiratory, integumentary (skin), musculo-skeletal, gastro-intestinal, genito-urinary, and the central nervous system. While we list these individual parts, all are interdependent and seek to operate in a state of homeostasis (or balance). What is relevant in this discussion is the *interrelationships* between the individual parts and the whole—the micro to the macro, and the informer, informing the system of what needs to change—feedback in pursuit of seeking balance.

Our lives crisscross a multi-layered network of complex systems in the course of a day. We are part of a family system, drive an automobile of intricate systems, go to work in a labyrinth of organizational systems, and communicate via multifaceted phones and computers (Do I need to discuss the complicated and convoluted inner workings of such?). We surf our "smart" TVs and appliances, and command our artificial intelligence to respond. Above all, I prefer taking a walk through nature's ecosystem.

While tending my garden, I unearthed similarities between the many businesses I had analyzed when the parallels emerged between theories I had applied to evaluate organizations and the plants and nature around me.

Searching for the correct remedy for a wilting plant, the answer might appear simple: lack of nutrients, too much or too little water, or perhaps a pest infestation caused not only by poor soil but disharmony in the larger environment. Could the affliction be a result of harmful pesticides that have killed off natural predators?

The interrelationships of nature's ecosystem: plant type, soil, location and the micro/macro associations, the volatility and vulnerabilities are reminiscent of my experiences as an emergency department nurse, where I was managing the multiple systems of patients and the operations of the department in a dynamic world where the emergency department (a microcosm of the hospital) echoed the intrinsic processes of the entire hospital (and the hospital, a microcosm of the overall healthcare delivery system's macrocosm).

Open vs. Closed System

Systems can be either open or closed. A truly closed system is difficult to imagine because it operates entirely independent of all external elements, utilizing its output as sustenance to keep the system operational. In other words, utilizing its outputs as inputs. (See system diagram) Can you think of a truly closed system? On the other hand, a system may appear closed and intact— such as the circulatory system—but it cannot exist without oxygen and other essential external components and is therefore clearly an open system.

Once again, using the human body as an example, each system may be treated by a specialist, for example a dermatologist, who sometimes is so focused that consideration of the relative nature of the skin to the rest of the other systems may be ignored. Each system contributes to the overall integrity of the organism. A break in the skin can introduce bacteria into the entire system, and, if deep and unchecked, can lead to sepsis and death. This may seem like an extreme illustration, but we can usually see that true healing occurs when considering the entire system. In the human body, the entire organism is viewed as the "macro" system, and the individual parts are the "micro" system.

Similarly, a break in the bark of an oak tree by the pernicious beetle is an entranceway to complete destruction of the tree. This annihilating beetle will not attack a healthy tree, only one that is otherwise compromised. Both the skin and bark of a tree represent one entrance to a set of complex multiple systems.[64]

The concept of macro versus micro is relative. For example, our skin and organs are further broken down into tissue, tissue into cells, cells into molecules, molecules into atoms and on into the most elemental particles. So, you see, an organ could be macro to more rudimentary micro parts, and, of course, the human body is a microcosm of the human race.

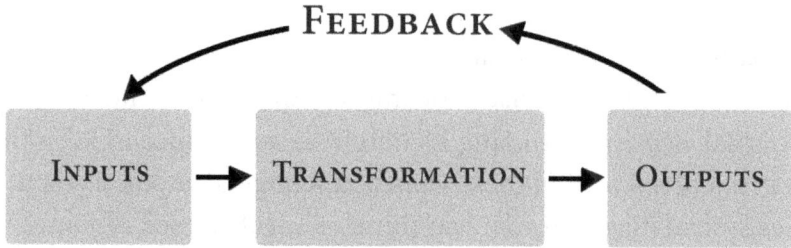

Systems can be simple or complex, but all systems operate with a three-part process: *inputs that are transformed into outputs*. Adjustments are constantly made through the process of *feedback*. Seeds, with the help of water and sun, are transformed and become a plant. A set of words become an essay, thread becomes a dress, two cells become a human, row crops become a yield that feeds millions, several people transform an idea into a business, and a couple create generations of ancestors.

Like humans, traversing life's precipice, constantly seeking balance, so too, plants adjust to their smaller, micro, and larger, macro environment for equilibrium or homeostasis. Whenever nature is out of balance, such as in times of drought, plants will compensate for a period of time—either they will adapt or die. Moving away from the simple example of a system with inputs that are transformed to outputs and maintain homeostasis through a feedback system, let's move on to explore *complex systems*—an infinite number of independent systems becoming interdependent.

A simple phone call to customer service has become a complex transaction created by a chain of algorithms. We live in a world of interdependent, intricate systems used in our day-to-day lives: cell phones, laptops, car engines, scores of applications we depend on, all leaving us vulnerable to slight shifts of change—a single disruption within a micro system will impact all the other parts of the complex interconnected macro system.

Some of the more difficult business systems to manage are those that have an unpredictable, on-demand aspect, such as fast food or the emergency department. Such systems can change their requirement for human resources at any moment. To predict needed resources, we look at past trends and staffing, and plan according to historical/ retrospective data.

When consulting for hospitals and emergency rooms, I suggested that the *supply* of inpatient rooms be staffed and available based upon trends in *demand* to anticipate and remove potential barriers in patient movement. I could never understand why admissions from the emergency department to the critical care areas seemed unexpected when, day after day, a push or demand for an average number of beds was a constant. Sure, the demand may change somewhat, however, based upon collected data, and benchmarked against similar hospitals, the requests for a certain number of beds was predictable. So why were patients waiting long hours in the emergency department for an inpatient bed? I suggested that when a patient was admitted, their discharge planning begin at the same time—a methodology to keep the system moving forward to meet new demand for beds. After all, the continuous turnover in beds created more open/empty beds, preventing barriers to overall flow within the hospital's system. Of course, caring for patients is a dynamic process, yet, too often a failure to manage patient turnover is a macro system problem. Federal policy has created a safety net in our emergency departments; emergency departments are open to all-comers, *everyone* no matter their ability to pay. When a system is pushed over an extended period, it pushes back.

Throughout my years managing people and consulting, I would impart a resounding admonition: Everything you do has an effect on someone or something. There is a cause and effect to every action we take or choose not to take.

Reflect in Your Garden

As you move through a single day, consider every system you encounter. Make a list of the multitude of systems you engage in daily.

Consider just one of the systems you encounter and think about how all the parts of the system are interrelated.

As you enjoy the extraordinary and complex world of nature, observe the interrelationships between each element you see, touch, smell and wrap all your senses around.

Focus on a single task you perform daily. Now, jot down every person and each part of this process necessary to complete this single task.

CAUSE AND EFFECT AND FEEDBACK LOOPS

Throughout my years managing people and consulting, I would impart a resounding admonition, *everything you do has an effect on someone or something. There is a cause and effect to every action we take or choose not to take.*

Once again, the human body is an excellent example of the concept of maintaining equilibrium within a system. Should the system become out of balance from a lack of water, oxygen and essential nutrients, the system seeks homeostasis. Daily, we experience thirst, hunger, fatigue, and millions of chemical reactions giving our brains feedback as to what our body needs to remain stable. The involuntary action of breathing occurs in a cause-effect reaction when the brain is alarmed by a drop in oxygen causing us to inspire. In turn, inspiration triggers a build-up of carbon dioxide signaling our brains to expire. If we hold our breath, run too long or submerge underwater, such activities send signals to the brain (feedback) to make adjustments—or we die.

The human body is a complex system of interrelated systems that are interdependent upon every other system to survive. Hunger, thirst, fatigue, blood pressure, and all of our senses are interdependent on the variabilities of the infinite indicators that move in response to waves of irregularities and inconsistencies pushing us to adapt and maintain stability.

We need knowledge of our plant to diagnose the cause of the symptoms and how to affect change. A wilting plant likely needs water, fertilizer or to be moved out of the sun. In business, the adjustments may not be life-threatening but can still jeopardize the solvency of the company. Poor quality, which often results from poor communication, are two common root causes of the demise of a business.

ENTROPY

Have you ever entered your garage and looked around with exasperation at the chaos—the mess that seems to engulf you? What you're enmeshed in is the result of entropy. Without the input of energy to keep a system in order, the system will return to a state of disorder. It is the natural tendency of things to lose order. Left to its own devices, life will always become less structured. Sand castles get washed away. Weeds overtake gardens. Ancient ruins crumble. Cars begin to rust. People gradually age. Ice melts, sugar dissolves, and given enough time, even mountains erode and their precise edges become rounded. The inevitable trend is that things become less organized. Systems are dynamic with constant change.

The universe is expanding with the added energy from entropy.[65] This is a fact. No business or garden is sustainable without the input of energy in the form of human or natural resources.

PROBLEM-SOLVING WITHIN A SYSTEM AND CAUSE AND EFFECT

Recall the four parts of a system: the input, transition, output and feedback that tells the system when it's out of balance. As discussed in the prior section, consider the idea that each part of the system can be used as a springboard to problem-solving, and, if left unchecked, a means of destroying even the most complex system.

Problems can be solved at every phase of the system. Deconstructing a system into its individual parts is essential; however, an understanding of the *interrelationships* between the parts is integral to identifying the root cause of a problem—the first step to a solution.

LONG WAITS: CAUSE AND EFFECT

The problem of excessive wait times in the emergency department was an ever-present issue. Let's look at segregating the *inputs/patients*, into specialized categories, versus all patients being placed on the same "conveyor belt" heading toward *transformation/wellness*, into the *output/release from the hospital*. Why have a patient who has had a sore throat for three weeks waiting with the football player with a compound, displaced leg fracture, and difficult to diagnose patients complaining of a headache and abdominal pain? A shift in thinking is needed to let go of the old and create a new, more efficient system—segregating the non-urgent from the more serious patients. The new way of thinking is to divide the system into two parts—more and less urgent. The inputs are therefore segregated to more efficiently transform the ill patient into a treated patient.

Today, these two-level acuity systems are now part of the emergency delivery system; however, such non-acute, "walk-in" or "rapid care" sections weren't always the norm. We can look at any part of a system to improve efficiencies to the output. Next, let's break down an even more complex system, expanding on the example above.

In the prior section, we segregated the *inputs* as a means of reducing wait times. Now let's look at how we can manage the *transformation process* to reduce wait times. This part of the patients' experience occurs once they pass the input portion of the process to the transformative part—discharged to an inpatient bed or released. In one community hospital's emergency department, working with the medical and nursing director, we brought every stakeholder to the table who touched the patient during their short or long emergency department stay to discharge—out the door or to an inpatient bed. This team not only included emergency department nurses and doctors, but administration, housekeeping, lab technicians, and nurses from critical care areas, with an objective to improve the time it took for a patient coming through the door to leaving. We broke down each minute and each step a patient took before seeing a physician, nurse practitioner or physician assistant.

We spent months correcting the *input process*: reducing the times patients spent at each station such as registration, triage, or waiting for lab results. Our work concluded with the patient in front of a physician in fifteen minutes—the same time spent previously to simply register a patient. We reduced every interdepartmental visit to and from the emergency department, including the time to admit patients from the emergency department to an inpatient bed. By looking at the problem from the input (patient seeking care) to transformation (needed care) to output (treated patient), and as a multifunctional team effort, the end result was a sustainable correction to all parts of the system. The results of such efforts were exceeding industry standards for immediate and quality care.

How did we accomplish such astonishing success? First, we identified each element in the entire system: inputs, the transformation process and outputs, and how each part of the system was *interrelated*. Second, we began to place controls on the elements that impacted each step within the system. We measured the time at every stage of *transformation*: the times it took for patients to be moved to each part of the hospital from the ED, such as X-ray and lab (the macro system), then back to the ED (the micro system), and finally, discharged home or to an inpatient bed. We collected data for 90 days, identifying and measuring constraints in care. We then investigated the root cause of each delay. For example, we found patients waiting 12 hours for an in-patient bed to be ready/available to transfer the patient. We found the cause to be anything from the bed not being cleaned to a nurse not being called-in—an effort to save costs of care. We found patients lingering in beds because they could not produce urine for a test, or a patient's X-ray delayed an hour because they were not properly undressed when the technician came to escort them. We had to identify not only the steps each patient took during their overall treatment, but what barriers to care were occurring, and how to remove these barriers. Each action within the macro has a cause and effect, as does each inaction.

> *I summarize the causes of the high cost of health care (the effect) into the "Five Ps": patient demand, policies, pharmaceutical costs, providers' practice of defensive medicine and (payors) payment system.*

In the above example of patient wait times, we not only identified the immediate cause: a bed not being available, but delved deeper to get to the root cause. We learned beds were not available for a patient to be transferred to an inpatient bed because a room sat uncleaned. The room was not clean because the housekeeping staff not only had the habit of all going on dinner break together, but had only half the workforce of the dayshift, which ended at 4:00 p.m. Yet, after 4:00 p.m. was when most of the admissions from the emergency department occurred. Second, we learned the nursing supervisors were encouraged to wait until the night shift, starting at 11:00 p.m., to call in another in-patient nurse as a cost-saving alternative. Because nurse managers and supervisors were heavily reprimanded for being over budget, each nursing department was trying to keep their budget down and left patients in the emergency department to place the cost of care under the emergency department's budget. We then learned the tight budgets were, in part, due to the underfunding of patient care. Hospitals offset some of this underfunding through their tax- exempt status—exchanging the provision of charity care for tax relief. For years, and to some extent continuing today, hospitals charge insured patients more to offset the patients who do not pay. However, this practice of "cost-shifting" has lessened since the advent of managed care—the cost burden weighs heavily on taxpayers and those who pay for healthcare.

Consider how many systems a single patient encounters in order to receive care in the emergency department? When you hear the adage "it's a system failure" how far-reaching is "the system"? To find a sustainable solution, each system within the healthcare delivery system, including the federal policymakers, to the microsystem or emergency department, needs to be identified and a root cause exposed. However, one can see that drilling down to the core of all the interrelated sub-systems within a more complex, overarching system, is onerous due to the innumerable variables. When I was a professor of health policy teaching a class of doctoral students in healthcare, I summarized the causes of the high cost of health care (the effect) into the "Five Ps": patient demand, policies, pharmaceutical costs, providers' practice of defensive medicine and (payors) payment system.

Let us look at another example of problem-solving in a less complex environment of out-patient care, addressing the significance of "cause and effect." An elderly patient arrived to a medical practice for a procedure. She was placed in the exam room, and, as the doctor began the procedure, it was learned a necessary solvent wasn't available. The *cause*: the last medical assistant to use the solvent failed to order and restock this liquid. The *effect*: the patient, an 85- year-old woman, had to be rescheduled, including her ride; expense of staff and other operating costs rose, and the physician lost income. I was most concerned about the inconvenience caused to any patient, but especially this patient. For all of you reading this who care for an elderly parent or patient, you know how difficult getting to a doctor's appointment can be, especially in the gridlocked south San

Francisco Bay area. This oversight was an excellent opportunity for the entire staff to learn how each one of their actions, and inactions, impacted so many.

I think we can all imagine showing up to the doctor's office for a procedure, then having to wait. An infinite number of causes can lead to this issue. A single event, such as a patient arriving late, or physician taking too long in a patient exam, can cause a ripple effect.

Let's venture away from the emergency department and into the vast outside world.

MORE ON CAUSE AND EFFECT

Few people realize the causes that impact the cost of goods sold—a cost that affects us all. Fuel prices affect nearly every commodity consumers touch. Lawsuits lead to higher insurance costs, leading to rising business costs passed on to consumers. Natural disasters such as fires, hurricanes and earthquakes increase the costs of insurance and services that, in turn, are passed on to consumer goods. Bankruptcies translate to losses for creditors who must recoup those losses by charging the next customers more. Every tax and expensive regulation is a business expense passed on to shoppers. The fewer people that pay, the greater the burden on those that do pay. Such incremental taxes pose a more significant impact on many fixed-income seniors.

Now let's move on to a discussion of the infinite causes and effects that have impacted our vast ecosystem.

Cause and Effect: My Garden, Your Garden and Our Interrelated World

Mother Nature deserves more respect. I am saddened thinking about the 80 million kilograms of plastic consumed by the living species inhabiting what was a marine sanctuary. Described in a June 25, 2019 article that identifies this plastic highway as the "Great Pacific Garbage Project" (GPGP),[66] which spans a distance comparable to three countries the size of France laid side by side. These synthetic polymers consist of 1.8 trillion pounds of grocery bags, bottles, personal packaging, and more, floating in the Pacific Ocean.[67] Can you conjure a more profound example of human hedonism causing such a deleterious effect on our sacred environment? Where do we begin to solve the cause and effect on this vast 155 million square kilometer aquatic system—the largest and deepest water mass in our precious ecosystem?

The logical, perhaps knee-jerk, response is to limit the amount of plastic by placing a cost at the input phase of the system in order to decrease the excessive amount of plastic used. However, have we really gotten to the root cause of the problem? Let us look deeper at the cause and effect of plastic upon our Pacific Ocean system.

I'm a Little Confused; Is This a Paradox?

In an effort to reduce the incidence of AIDS and hepatitis, as far back as 2013, Santa Cruz County, California, distributed 20,000 needles in one month, with that number doubling and tripling since. In 2020, San Francisco County distributed 5.8 million syringes with an estimated 90,000 collected in a six-month period; in the year prior two million of the five million were collected. In addition to a projected need of 12 million needles a year, of which San Francisco's Health Department would like to meet, burning pans, tourniquets and cotton balls are also disseminated without an organized process of collection.[68] Used needles are found in parks, beaches and scattered over streets that, not only unsuspecting residents are subjected to, but the millions of worldwide tourists that come to enjoy these iconic cities. Innocent people are exposed to the very diseases intended for eradication. Such unintended consequences are the result of trying to solve a problem within a complex system without identifying and remediating the root cause.

These same Pacific Coast counties have banned plastic straws and implemented a twenty-five-cent fee for a plastic bag or cup—an effort to reduce plastic contamination in the Pacific Ocean.[69] I find this push-pull effort a paradox. We remove the use of plastic straws and introduce thousands of plastic contaminants impaling barefooted beach lovers and scattering disease-borne pollutants on the streets of the same counties.[70] Cause and effect and the unintended consequences—all interconnected.

Necklace of Green Jewels

You embrace me—
like a necklace of green jewels
pine, cedar, fir and eucalyptus
the stalwart palm erect and regal

Your dress is home to starlings
crows and the mighty hawks—
perched and cloaked in the
scent and firmness of your arms.

Clouds gather, filled with earth's nectar.
Tempestuous winds unfurl and you listen—
do the gusts command you to sing
or chant a hymn of dominance?

Will you spread a veil for the vulnerable
or squash new life as your roots erupt?
Will you amass your power to embrace
the minimal plants and feral creatures

seeking refuge beneath you?
When my soul separates
and I bathe on the waves near you—
where the ashes of my last life are scattered,

I'll perch on a branch and listen—
listen as you assure me
animals and fish are free of debris, and—
earth has been cleansed of man's harm.

AT THE INTERSECTION OF CAUSE AND EFFECT— ALL LIVING THINGS ARE INTERCONNECTED

Every spade of the earth I turn has a cause and effect beyond the boundaries of my garden—one that impacts the birds, deer, ground squirrels, insects, and all that live nearby and visit. My garden and your garden are interrelated in this grand ecosystem we share.

In the autumn of 2020, four million acres of California burned. The cause of this unprecedented disaster is attributed to climate change. And what is the root cause of climate change? Before humans existed, forests were naturally maintained. Animals roamed free to innately dispose of the forest's debris—Mother Nature's method of naturally pruning plant wastes and dead trees in order to provide space for new growth. Human intervention utilizing controlled burns and clearing overgrown brush are means of being good stewards of our woodlands, plants and animal life.[71]

Cause and Effect: Drugs and the World's Waterways

I don't think we can educate the populace enough as to the cause and effect of putting pollutants into the earth and the impact on living systems through the food chain. My research related to plastic in our waterways led me to an equally disturbing discovery of pollutants—heroin and cocaine—spreading their byproducts into the mouths and stomachs of our fish and marine mammals. Delving deeper, I uncovered research related to toxins in our world's rivers, streams, canals and all watercourses. The article, *Cocaine and Heroin in Wastewater Plants: a-year study of Florence, Italy,*[72] documents testing wastewater treatment plants as a means of measuring drug use in a specific population. However, a 2014 article in the *Independent*, "Cocaine Use So High in Britain It has Contaminated Drinking Water,"[73] details evidence of these drugs even after "intensive purification" through their wastewater treatment plants. While authorities conclude the amounts are below therapeutic levels and not a public health risk, what other risks do these findings portend? A similar case is said for Italy's longest river, the River Po, that traverses Turin, Milan, Lombardy and flows on to the Adriatic Sea.[74] Eels in the River Thames are increasingly hyperactive and their populations on the decline; one reason is due to cocaine inhibiting them from travel to reproduce. Upon dissection of the intoxicated eels, cocaine was found in their brains, gills and muscles.[75] The cause is apparent, the effects are far reaching into Mother Nature's aquatic children—and then where?

Your garden, my garden and earth—we're all interrelated as one magnificent system.

Reflect in Your Garden

Reflect on Edward Lorenz' concept of a butterfly's wings impacting the weather on the other side of the earth.

Take a moment to consider all the complex systems you are surrounded by and use on a daily basis.

When one of these complex systems fails to accomplish the task it was designed to do, what corrective action do you take?

Identify one problem (effect) you face in the garden of your life, and make a list of all the causes. How have you been part of the cause? What are you going to do to remediate the causes?

How might you be part of the cause in the destruction of someone else's garden?

Product Failures: Cause and Effect

In order to solve a problem in any system you have to understand how all the parts within the macrosystem are *interrelated*. Simply identifying all the parts (microsystems) of the macrosystem is not enough, you must understand how the parts communicate—the cause and effect of each single part on the whole system. Let's look at the impact of a company's failure to maintain product quality.

General Electric (GE) released a refrigerator with a rotary compressor that is an example of design failure.[76] I had the misfortune of owning one of these products and, thanks to my astute appliance repairman, I was able to get a new compressor at no expense. I didn't say "at no cost" but "no expense." My repairman had seen numerous cases of this failure and informed me that GE had knowledge of the design failure with the resultant 100 percent failure rate, yet the product was released to the market. The Groupthink (see Chronology of Organizational Theory, Chapter 6) among decision-makers kept the knowledge of a potential failure from being remedied.

The American auto industry went from being the world's number one manufacturer of cars in the 1950s and 60s. In his book, *Detroit: An American Autopsy*, the author, Charlie LeDuff writes:

> "...once the richest city in America, Detroit is now the nation's poorest. ...Once the vanguard of America's machine age—mass production, blue-collar jobs, and automobiles—Detroit is now America's capital for unemployment, illiteracy, dropouts, and foreclosures...deserted factories, abandoned homes and forgotten people."[77]

> *Detroit turned out to be heaven, but it also*
> *turned out to be hell.*
>
> —Marvin Gaye

Production and Project Management: Cause and Effect

The quality of a product is insured at the design and testing phases. There is no place for an imperfect prototype being sent off to manufacturing, or a failure to identify sources of poor quality during the design and testing phase. However, the more complex the system and the more we outsource parts (input) of a complex product, the greater likelihood a product defect will be overlooked before being released to the marketplace. Once again, we must understand the interrelationship of all the parts of the whole to ensure excellence in the output: superior input, superior construction (transformation) of all the input should ensure a superior output, however, testing and retesting (the feedback element of the system) must be undertaken until a flawless product is released. Conversely, without exceptional service to deliver and support these products, the business will suffer.

The following diagram illustrates the relationship between value, quality and cost. Real value comes from producing a quality product that is well serviced and sold at a relatively low cost. The Japanese entrance into auto production put the American automakers on notice that a low-cost, high-quality vehicle could be produced.

Formula for Value

$$V = \frac{Q + S}{C}$$

Where V is value, Q is quality, S is service/support and C is cost/price.

To better understand this concept of improving products and efficiencies at every part of a process, let's look at two types of project management styles—the traditional Waterfall Method and Agile Project Management[78]—using a newly-designed hospital bed as our project under development.[79]

In the Waterfall Method, the hospital bed would be designed in phases in a sequential process at the input stage of our system. Each phase is finished before the next phase of design is completed, as the project moves forward without returning to an earlier phase. A great deal of effort would be made to construct a perfect prototype, then manufactured and marketed. In Agile Project Management, the hospital bed would be developed according to the designer's and manufacturer's vision of the ideal bed for the market, however, in this process, the bed would be repeatedly market tested with feedback from the end-users. Multiple market tests would be conducted with numerous iterations of the bed design after each market test, until a perfect prototype was created. Agile Project Management evolved to better support the development and testing of software for release without defects, and to ensure the deliverable meets the customers' expectations.

When embarking on a project there is a triad of interdependent considerations: time, cost, and scope. Overarching all three is quality (see diagram) and illustrates the importance of acute oversight by the project manager to monitor all the variables and know when trade-offs or compromises are necessary to ensure a successful outcome.

The diagram below illustrates the interdependence among the variables of price, time, scope and quality.

Quality is Overarching

Scope   Time

Price

All are necessary, but one is often compromised for the other two. If you want a plumber on Sunday you will likely spend more. When undertaking a business project on a fixed budget, you may want to put tight constraints on the length of the project and pay special attention to the scope and quality of output. The quality of the project is overarching this triangle of factors, and as the scope of the project expands so will the cost and length of the project. How often do you hear "We have expanded the project's deliverables but want to stay on budget, on time and maintain a high-quality outcome?" Or,"Human and monetary resources have been cut but we still need to have the project completed in less time with zero defects." Is a successful project outcome tenable?

COMPLEXITY THEORY: CAUSE AND EFFECT ARE NOT ALWAYS LINEAR

Chaos Theory and Complex Adaptive Theory are part of Complexity Theory. In the previous sections I gave examples of cause and effect in a linear framework—if plotted on an x and y graph creates a straight line. However, in nonlinear systems such as those described in chaos theory and complex adaptive systems (CAS), you would find the change in the amount of output is not proportional to the change in the amount of input. Growth in such systems can happen quickly, unpredictably, and according to its own set of rules. CAS may behave based on chance.[80] Examples of CAS include the developing embryo, the human brain, ant colonies, traffic, the immune system, the economy and ecosystem.

Complex Adaptive Systems

Complex adaptive systems (CAS) are made up of many individual parts and are nonlinear, spontaneous, and small changes can lead to significant results. Change is not only constant, but rapid and normal. Bringing together a diverse set of systems typically creates a predictable outcome with the sum total greater than the sum of the parts (see High Performing Teams, Chapter 6), however, the systems in CAS adapt, mutate and self-organize, ultimately leading to an unpredictable outcome. Such systems can be a single cell or an entire organism. Complex adaptive systems are without a leader, self-organizing and form emergent patterns without being directed to do so.

John Holland is considered the pioneer in the study of complex adaptive systems, beginning his career at IBM in the 1950s. In his extraordinary book, *Adaptation in Natural and Artificial Systems: An Introductory Analysis with Applications to Biology, Control, and*

Artificial Intelligence, he describes how climate, cells and traffic are examples of complex adaptive systems.[81]

Complex adaptive systems have been characterized as "stochastic" or governed by chance. These systems are dynamic, ever changing and adapt to continuous external change, thus generating uncertainty in the systems' outcome. Are some plants and business organizations subject to the same rules of continuous change; adapting to the fluctuations of internal and external forces, thus making predicting outcomes indeterminate and unstable?

Despite having taken calculus, my acumen for mathematics is diminutive relative to minds like John Holland's—I won't even try to present the mathematical derivation behind his theory of how complex systems adapt. Holland explained for us how complex systems can prepare for future survival—to actually prepare to survive in an environment without having previously lived in that environment. He explains how survival of a living thing depends on adaptation. Holland's work has been applied to the disciplines of economics, artificial intelligence and human and natural systems. Also in his book, *Adaptation of Natural and Artificial Systems*, Holland explains how systems, from a bacterium to a wolf, use "internal models" to anticipate the future. The systems that survive have been able to sift through millions or more pieces of information to keep only the bits that are needed to ward off predators in the future. Is it plausible plants ward off predators utilizing the same sorting and sifting for future protection and survival?

> *It is not the strongest of the species that survive, or the most intelligent, but the one most responsive to change.*
>
> —Charles Darwin

Chaos Theory

Chaos Theory also has a mathematical foundation first documented by Henri Poincare. Poincare is considered to be one of the greatest mathematicians of all time, contributing to the theory of differential equations, electromagnetism, topology and the philosophy of mathematics. He undertook numerous unfinished research projects including chaos theory. Edward Lorenz, a Professor of Meteorology at Massachusetts Institute of Technology, who had studied Poincare, deduced from his formulations that small changes in complex systems can cause extreme changes in the greater or macro system. Commonly known as the Butterfly Effect, Lorenz described how the flapping of the wings of a butterfly in one part of the world can cause a hurricane in another part of the world. This is Chaos Theory, which explains that all living things want to survive, but only the fittest and most adaptable survive. Chaos Theory illustrates that external competition is not typical because survival is of the fittest and the system itself must adapt to its environment to last. Not only does the system seek survival but must do so efficiently and effectively—continuously improving itself![82] The urge to compete is self-generated.[83]

Chaos Theory relates to systems that are extremely sensitive to a change in a nearby system, making modifications to itself with an insignificant change in a related system, albeit distant or near. The weather is a good example of a system sensitive to slight change that may result in a substantial difference.[84]

Survival of the fittest is about competing with oneself to adapt and survive. While it seems a bit confusing or incongruent to what we may think, one system doesn't actually compete with other systems unless it needs some part of the other system. Applying this to organizations, its survival must come from an unremitting ability to improve its products and processes. Leadership must continuously change and improve itself from within.[85]

While we have finished with the topics of systems theory and complexity science for now, I will revisit the subjects in my discussion on COVID-19 following Chapter 6.

Chapter 6 will engage the reader in an overview of an array of topics related to the "people" side of operating a business. We will again embark upon uncovering the many parallels between nature and business.

CHAPTER 6

Organizational Theory

EXCUSE ME, BUT WHAT IS ORGANIZATIONAL THEORY?

W hen asked what I taught, I'd respond with *Organizational Theory*! and watch the person's eyes glaze over and observe the polite smile. Sometimes I'd wait for them to sheepishly walk away when my back was turned or say, *excuse me, but what is organizational theory?* To simplify the answer I'd merely reply, *oh, it's how organizations/businesses are designed to communicate, to create change, to lead and build teams—the people side of the organization.* Shoulders would relax and the glazed eyes would soften to demonstrate a better understanding. *I'm writing about the parallels of nature to business.* The perplexed look returns; this time I see a creeping desperation as they look for the nearest exit. Perhaps you'll humor me by reading on.

Organizational theory encompasses the design and structure of a business, as well as the behavior brought to the organization by its human resources, and includes leadership and group dynamics. Overlapping the subsets of leadership and group dynamics are culture and communication. Group dynamics includes such topics as team building, conflict, negotiation and a multitude of communication issues within an organization. Organizational development is a discipline that brings together the design and behavior of the organization in order to accomplish an enterprise or company-wide change effort. I believe that without strong leadership, adequate resources and support for the human resources, no long-lasting change will occur.

Many people are unfamiliar with organizational theory as its applications are not often taught with the core business courses of finance, economics and accounting, albeit more business programs now include such a course. Organizational theory is commonly disregarded, or thought of as the "soft" side of business since it is not directly associated with the financial health of a company. Ironically, the human resources and leadership can severely impact the strengths of an organization, just as pervasive crabgrass will overtake an entire lawn.

> *The human resources and leadership can severely impact the strengths of an organization, just as crabgrass overtakes an entire lawn.*

I had attained my doctorate and had been teaching organizational theory for several years when I undertook the Master of Information Systems (MSIS) Program at the University of San Francisco. I caught the attention of the program director while giving a presentation on the genesis of many organizational theories, derived by the early contributors to computer science and information technology. As a result, she asked me to develop a course in organizational theory for the graduate and undergraduate information systems curriculums. I both designed and taught the course for years, gleaning firsthand the dearth of awareness most technologists have of the organization's design, development and behavior. Technologists are not the only employees unaware of the overall business outside of their work area. Most employees know the immediate surroundings and processes of their department, however, typically these employees have little concept of the inner workings and interrelationships between the many systems within an organization.

I had two goals as an educator: First, to inspire my students to think critically, to question and delve deep into scientific research for the answers. Second, to leave the classroom with the ability to *apply* organizational theory in their workplace. I was a better educator because I brought real-world application from my consulting practice into the classroom, and, in turn, I was a better consultant because I had in-depth knowledge of the underlying theory behind the recommendations I made to clients. I have included a chapter dedicated to organizational theory to not only introduce you to the concepts, but to find relevance and application in your business or personal life.

You may be asking yourself what organizational theory and business have to do with nature—after all, isn't that what this book is about? Nature and its ecosystem are grand systems composed of millions of smaller complex bodies. Business organizations mimic nature with similarities such as inputs from the internal and external environment, a transformative process of the inputs into outputs, and a means of maintaining balance. Businesses, like nature, are composed of smaller units competing for resources, with an infinite number of causes and effects, pushes and pulls on the system, seeking homeostasis through balancing and reinforcing loops. Nature's vast macro and infinite micro systems have many more innate powers to self-regulate than businesses. Nature doesn't need endless meetings, project managers or to wait for resource approvals to get the job done. Perhaps we need a corporate structure fashioned after nature's ability to stabilize.

Businesses, like nature, are composed of smaller units, each competing for resources, with an infinite number of causes and effects, pushes and pulls on the system, seeking homeostasis through balancing and reinforcing loops.

CHRONOLOGY OF ORGANIZATIONAL THEORY

In order to appreciate the evolution of organizations today, it is important to know the history behind the design, development and behavior, including leadership, of such entities of the past. Let's look at some of those who contributed to building the base of knowledge we refer to as organizational theory.

Organizations were designed after the structure of the church and military—the only two examples of formal organizations hundreds of years ago when organizational theory was first introduced. The first documented account of organizational theory is 1491 B.C., when Jethro, father-in-law to Moses, urged Moses to delegate authority over the tribes of Israel, creating a hierarchy of leadership. In 500 B.C. Socrates argued for management as an art.[86]

In 1776, Adam Smith wrote *The Wealth of Nations*, introducing the concept of division of labor. Francis Galton, in his 1869 book, *Hereditary Genius*, concluded in his trait theory that leaders were born with innate characteristics that cannot be developed or taught—considered plausible even today. In 1911, Frederick Winslow Taylor published *The Principles of Scientific Management*,[87] introducing efficient practices into the workplace. In 1916, Henri Fayol published "General and Industrial Management," the first complete theory of management—his 14 principles of management are still applicable today. Mary Parker Follett's, "The Giving of Orders," remains a respected commentary on how effective leaders should communicate.[88]

The military began research in the early 1930s in an effort to match an individual's assigned work with their skills and abilities. But it would be nearly 20 years before businesses would adopt a similar philosophy.

Organizational theory began to grow in popularity post-World War II, when companies saw a relationship between the skill set an individual brought to the company and his/her success at a given job. Except for those at the top, companies had a unilateral relationship with an individual worker. Prior to this time workers were seen as a commodity to perform a single function, as in the assembly line. Moving into the 1950s and '60s, companies began to study the behavior of workers, their motivations, and how to garner optimal productivity from individuals and groups. In 1943, Abraham Maslow published his hierarchy of needs and its associated theories of human motivation. The 1950s introduced many long-standing theories and concepts by such noted researchers as Kurt Lewin, Chris Argyris, Ludwig Von Bertanffy and Norbert Weiner. Peter Drucker garnered the well-deserved title as the "father of management" for his contributions over nearly 50 years. Irving Janis launched the concept of Groupthink, patterns of behavior exposed in unusual or situations of extraordinary high stress. Chester Barnard uncovered the concept of the informal organization in the 1970s. In 1979, Henry Mintzberg described the *Five Basic Parts of the Organization*: the strategic, or apex; middle, or middle management; operating core, or the group of individuals considered the line workers; with two arms including technostructure (scanning the environment) and support staff, including all ancillary workers such as legal, research and development, food service, payroll, public relations and more.[89]

Also, in the 1970s and '80s, Paul Hersey and Ken Blanchard's Situational Theory[90] suggested leaders emerge as a result of the events of the time. Edward Deming, author of *Quality Productivity and Competitive Position, Out of the Crisis (1982-1986)*, was instrumental post-World War II working with the Japanese to rebuild Japan structurally and help create what became a global economic powerhouse. His work was the genesis of the 1980s and '90s quality movement in the United States. William Bennis' books, *Leadership* and *On Becoming a Leader*[91] contributed extensively to the subjects of leadership and group dynamics. The 1980s brought *Organizational Culture and Leadership,* by Edgar Schein,[92] and Rosabeth Moss Kanter's "participation management" in *The Change Masters: Innovation for Productivity in the American Corporation.*[93] In the 1990s Peter Senge published *The Fifth Discipline*, introducing the concept of a learning organization.[94] Michael Porter, Harvard educated in economics and business, is known internationally for his contributions on strategy and competition. In his March 1979 *Harvard Business Review* article, "How Competitive Forces Shape Strategy,"[95] Porter introduced his Model of Five Forces.[96]

By no means is this a complete list, but an overview of the chronology of organizational theory; contributions to this field of research continue to this day.

ORGANIZATIONAL DESIGN/STRUCTURE AND DEVELOPMENT

An organization's design determines how communication and decision-making occur. In general, two business structures exist with permutations of each. Start-ups are flat, "organic" organizations that support centralized decision making, free-flowing communication and shared resources. In contrast are "mechanistic," bureaucratic structures that separate into product divisions, silos, or functional areas. Mechanistic designs are hierarchical with centralized decision-making and top-down communication, modeled after the ancient religious and soldierly command and control styles of interaction. Henri Fayol refers to this exchange of information through a rigid "chain of command."[97]

Today's organizations purport to have decentralized decision-making; however, too often this is an ideal as opposed to a reality. In the 21st century, complex organizations are a hybrid of designs, such as a matrix design in which an individual will report to a functional manager and department manager. An example of a matrix structure is an emergency department nurse reporting to both the nursing department and emergency department. Many companies have designs that are without any communication boundaries due to intranets, internet and cross-functional teams.

Organizational design has been used as a means of control and power. Let's use Apple as a hypothetical example. Since we are familiar with its product lines, let's imagine each of Apple's products are a division with all the needed functions to create and manage a single product line: iPad division, MacBook division, iPhone division and desktop division. Let's now imagine every one of these divisions has an executive leader, its own research and development, manufacturing, sales, marketing, accounting, human resources, and all the resources needed internal to its division. Under the guise of a money-saving reorganization, the Board and CEO now require the iPad division to combine resources with the iPhone division. Suddenly, the iPad executive has lost some of his/her responsibilities and now must share resources with the iPhone division. Ouch! Redesigning organizations that remove resources and responsibilities from a manager or executive is one means of edging someone out of the company, or achieving other objectives—a chess move in the direction of checkmate.

I think this is a good time to discuss the bases of power.

Bases of Power

Defined by Bertrum Raven and Henry French, the five bases of power are: expert, legitimate, referent, coercive and reward.[98] A sixth, information power, was later added. The strength of a particular power is dependent on the need of one party in association with another party. For example, information power is only of significance if the recipient of the data actually wants the material from the holder of the information. Referent power is gained by association with people who hold or have access to individuals who have power. If you want an appointment with the CEO of Apple to pitch your product, their executive secretary suddenly becomes important to you. If you don't like Paul McCartney, a backstage pass to have your picture taken with him holds no power over you. Individuals closely associated with celebrities in all areas, from the Pope to the U.S. president, hold referent power. The Pope and U.S. president also hold legitimate and expert power, as evidenced by their elected positions. Police also possess legitimate power. Symbols of legitimate power are in titles, positions in the hierarchy, a prime office location, religious robes, uniforms, epaulettes, crowns and more. We all know what power by fear, under duress and coercion looks like. The dictator of a country, head of a drug cartel or Mafia don are prime examples of coercive power. An individual or organization disseminating rewards, whether the Nobel, Oscar, Pulitzer or granting a doctorate degree, holds significant power. As their professor, I'd tell my students that I held legitimate, expert and reward, and maybe even information, powers simultaneously (and I would watch their eyes roll).

ORGANIZATIONAL BEHAVIOR

The study of organizational behavior includes leadership, culture and group dynamics. Leadership is a broad topic on which I could write extensively but have abbreviated for purposes of this book. I will discuss some of the theories regarding leadership but invite you to enjoy a few vignettes on authentic leaders. I follow the discussion of leadership with the definition and examples of an organization's culture. A topic readers will be most familiar with is group dynamics—including communication, conflict, teams and team building. You will find the theory and application transferable to any interpersonal communication you endeavor in the course of a day.

LEADERSHIP

The question of whether leadership is innate or learned seems indeterminate. After much study I believe it is a combination of both. Many leaders emerge due to timing, such as Martin Luther King, Jr. His ability to lead would have been squelched in the 1900s, despite the need for change. A convergence of circumstances arise, such as those that led to the Civil Rights movement of the 1960s which made way for Martin Luther King, Jr. to surface as one of our great leaders. Franklin Roosevelt rose to prominence upon the horror of the Day of Infamy, and Mahatma Gandhi gained independence for India after a long-fought battle, only to face strife between two disparate religious factions. Most leaders develop skills as they amass increasing responsibility and authority, rising up through ranks and tiers over time. "Climbing the corporate ladder" is the idiom we associate with individuals as they rise in a stepwise manner from staff to executive.

Some define a leader as "having followers." Abraham Lincoln, John Kennedy, Barack Obama and Donald Trump are all iconic political leaders who amassed a following through their expert and charismatic power. Unfortunately, there are leaders who have assembled a following by imposing coercive power—such as Hitler, Mao, Stalin, Kim Il Sung, Castro and a litany of dictators.

Effective leaders are always scanning the competition and looking forward. In a teaching video on leadership, Jeff Bezos, in his early years as CEO of Amazon said, "You can sell something to anyone once, but it's the repeat business that sustains your organization." This is even truer today in this acutely competitive business environment.

Max Depree, son of the founder of Herman Miller Furniture, Holland, Michigan, and author of *Leadership is an Art* and *Leadership Jazz* promoted the idea of open communication. Unlike many organizations that purported to operate under such a concept, he succeeded in its execution. Max DePree was associated with fulfilling his leadership promises, not just espousing popular ideas. His books are a course for leaders who want to continuously learn and question how well they are performing, suggesting such questions: *When was the last time I called to thank you…when did I last call a customer to see how we're doing…how long ago was it that I last saw the products we sell actually being made?*[99] DePree espoused that leaders should look beyond ratios and quotas and embrace *the diversity of people's gifts and talents.* In doing so the leader, as well as co-workers, can be dependent on others' skills admitting "we cannot know or do everything."[100]

> *Why can't institutions encompass comfortably and constructively the normal range of human emotions and aspirations and triumphs and failures?* [101]
>
> *It seems to me that polishing gifts, such a crucial part of the work of a leader, could be called tuning oneself for life.*[102]
>
> —Max DePree

Leadership by Walking Around

I can't prune one of my cherished rose bushes without looking at every angle and into its center. I hand water my roses to not only control water flow, but inspect the plants and clear the surrounding area of diseased leaves, meanwhile providing this valuable asset with all it needs to flourish. How does a leader understand the needs of its customers and human resources if not actively engaged in the quality of its daily output at all levels of the organization? Tom Peters coined the term *management by walking around* (MBWA) in his best-selling book, *In Search of Excellence.*[103]

I find it astonishing that we need to tell managers and leaders to "walk around" their company—to engage staff at all levels to provide input. While minimal by comparison, I cannot imagine taking responsibility for the staff and patients under my purview without making an initial assessment at the beginning and several times during each shift as a charge nurse in an emergency department. Additionally, I have always asked for evaluations of my performance as a manager, consultant and educator for every engagement/course. Oh sure, my responsibility was a speck of sand by contrast to a multinational company, yet, I don't apologize for making a similar comparison. I am also reminded of looking outward in my garden and admiring the abundant deep purple and pink hydrangeas as I water from a distance, only to get close and find a trove of various weed plants embedding their offspring inside the center of the magnificent plant. Without my thorough investigation of all points of view, I am certain to overlook impending trouble and learning new ideas on how to remedy the issue. Effective leaders do extend their office to the manufacturing lines, distribution centers and store departments, engaging side-by-side employees and gathering feedback from the frontline staff.

How can you possibly know who and what you are managing without looking into the eyes of your employees and walking among the people you oversee? Costco's co-founder and former CEO, Jim Sinegal, learned warehouse selling at Priceclub, and held "service" as Costco's core value, not just proselytizing, but embedded into every aspect of day-to-day operations. He made a commitment to visit each store each year—to walk the floors, getting to know staff and learning firsthand about his customers.[104] He spent 200 days a year visiting his stores—the epitome of getting out of his office and "walking around." Jim Senigal embodies the traits of a successful leader and one of the archetypes of authentic leaders.[105]

How does one manage a garden without constant examination to ensure the health of their plants? I can't imagine sitting indoors with the expectation that my garden will thrive.

196

There are many leaders who walk the fields of their farms to check every crop daily, like Dick Peixoto, owner of Lakeside Organics, in Watsonville, California, or inspect their vast nurseries as Ralph Moore and David Austin once did (see section on Authentic Leaders).

Plaques for Poor Performance

Halls of business offices are lined with plaques displaying the years of service provided by past leaders. But how many empty promises and poor performers hang along those walls? Effective leaders impart their vision at every level of staff and align every position toward meeting this vision. Each staff member's performance outcomes should be tied to meeting the organization's mission and vision. Consulting with a leader, I asked, "What is your vision for the company?" He pointed to his head and said, "It's all up here." He felt it unnecessary to share his ideas with any of his reports. Within a year he lost all his top management. Without communicating a clear vision at every level and every employee playing a role in this vision, not only is the leader likely to fail to achieve his/her goals but alienate the very individuals who are entrusted with the task of achieving the company's objectives. A poor leader fails to communicate with his/her human resources the overarching direction of the company. Not only must a leader effectively communicate their vision but garner input from every level of staff to create buy-in.

Let me recount a memorable experience exemplifying the misalignment of one business leader's vision juxtaposed to the actual, day-to-day behavior among the staff. A 200-bed community hospital's vice president championed the goal of attaining the prestigious Malcolm Baldrige National Quality Award.[106] The award is given to organizations demonstrating excellence in quality improvement according to an extensive list of metrics, and, at this time, healthcare organizations had just been added to the list of qualifying sectors. The hospital spent years and extraordinary amounts of money attempting to achieve superior grades in every measurement, providing excellence in healthcare delivery at every level of the patient's experience.

> *There is nothing quite so useless as doing with great efficiency something that should not be done at all.*
>
> —Peter Drucker

The vice president who championed this effort was so focused on attaining this award, he failed to leave the executive suite to spend time "walking around" the units of the hospital, engaging those doing the real work in conversations about what resources would improve their patient care. After all, central to the Baldrige Award is the core value of excellence in the quality of the product or service between customers and employees. The champion of this hospital's effort was rarely seen by employees and had a reputation for *never* leaving his office. One telling example of this vice president's lack of visibility among the workforce was at a meeting with a number of doctors and this prophet of quality. One of the doctors who had worked full-time in the emergency department for over two years leaned over to me and inquired, *who is this person?* The executive vice president failed to even peruse the emergency department for years, and was a stranger to those working in the department most accessible to the community it served.

This is an example of being oblivious to reality and illuminates the disparity between illusion and verisimilitude. I remember walking the halls of this same hospital, along its row of placards touting its many tenets demonstrating staff and client support. However, a chasm existed between those who championed quality by looking for awards versus the many staff who touched patients throughout their workday—actually making the "quality" difference rather than the bravado expressed in a tidy list of metrics. I'm quite certain the Baldridge committee saw through the phoniness of the vice president's aspirations in contrast to the sincere caring of staff and the real work being accomplished.

AUTHENTIC LEADERSHIP

I taught leadership for over 10 years and studied the subject for 25 plus years. I have read many books on the subject, analyzed business cases on leaders from all sectors: political, religious, sports, military, music and business and uncovered two common qualities among effective leaders: *being authentic and taking time for reflection.* Countless leaders, especially of small businesses or start-ups, are successful because they don't succumb to adversity. For some, in fact, such "hitting the wall" lessons launched them forward, determined to do better. The individuals I write about below were pioneers in their fields, forged a path never tread before and were not dissuaded by naysayers. Authentic leaders followed no one but their passion, overcoming one obstacle after another. Some leaders opened doors for the first time to employees, created a diverse workforce or simply respected their employees as people first with families and an opinion they wanted to hear. Let's look at a small sample of authentic leaders and their representative companies.

Authentic Rosarians

A fascination with technology, its exponential advances, and the dream of being a young billionaire, seem to have overshadowed the far greater numbers of entrepreneur leaders who have left a rich legacy that fulfills a far greater need—a relationship with nature. Among a vast assemblage of skilled rosarians, two men have endowed my garden with the products of their life's work. I'm grateful to be one of the millions of recipients of their dedication, artistry and the gifts they have given to us all.

After 25 years of studying leaders I uncovered two common qualities among effective leaders: "being authentic" and "taking time for reflection."

Ralph Moore, considered the "father of miniature roses," founded Sequoia Nursery in Visalia, California in 1937.[107] Now let's imagine it is 1937 and for centuries rose lovers and romantics have adored the shrub and climbing roses. Yet, Ralph Moore had a vision for a tiny version of roses in America. His first hybridized miniature resulted from crossing a climber with a small shrub rose to produce the white-flowered Sierra Snowstorm in 1937. No market existed for such a rose but he persevered. I not only admire the output of Ralph Moore's genius but his tenacity. He spent 24 years creating his first "moss" rose, Goldmoss, the first in both miniature and shrub. His creativity and fascination with striped flowers, crossing Little Chief and No. 14 Stripe, gave us "Stars n Stripes"— just in time for the centennial year, 1976. Before roses as groundcover became popular, Ralph Moore created Red Creeper—also used as a miniature climber. When asked about his favorite rose he would say, *The one I haven't made yet; it's perfect.*[108]

When asked why he continued to work into his '90s, Ralph Moore's response was…

Why do I keep on with my rose breeding? What better reason than to create beauty to share with others? For love of a rose, I want to keep on as long as I hear that other drummer—so long as I can dream dreams—so long as my new roses can speak of the glory of God.[109]

Moore has afforded me years of happiness as a result of his compassion and skills hybridizing dozens of miniature roses. As a novice growing roses, I undertook spreading Ralph Moore's joy throughout my garden. I was drawn to his vast array of captivating miniature rose cultivars. I actually tried to buy one of every rose listed on his website. I literally went to bed with Sequoia Nursery's petite catalogue of tiny roses, checking off my choices and filling in the order forms. I couldn't wait for the box of three-inch pots to arrive. I not only admire Ralph Moore's brilliance and originality, but his heart. What a legacy Ralph Moore left us in his 102 years.

After collecting hundreds of Ralph Moore's miniatures, I came to know David Austin roses when visiting a friend's garden. I was immediately smitten with the old-fashioned, symmetrically-splayed petals and captivating scent. I just knew there was something extraordinary about these roses. I had to learn more!

In the 1940s, in Shropshire, England, David Austin turned a teenage inspiration into a lifelong career. Despite his father's discouragement, hanging out at a neighbor's nursery, a *Garden Illustrated* magazine and A.E. Bunyard's book, *Old Garden Roses*, collectively inspired Austin to pursue his passion. He cherished the Old English rose, but the hybrid tea was growing in popularity. As a hobby, David Austin set out to create a rose with the fragrance and beauty of the Old English rose with the positive attributes of the hybrid teas— their spectrum of color and repeat bloom. But it would be another twenty years before his first hybrid, "Constance Spry," was created in 1960. His success was met with resistance from the marketplace, but Austin met this new challenge by selling his roses directly from the nursery.[110]

David Austin, considered the "father of the English Rose," has cultivated over 200 glorious roses, increasingly weather hardy and disease resistant over time.

My favorite is Pat Austin, the yellow-orange cupped beauty, but my garden is home to over 100 of David Austin's array of roses, and of this writing, I plan to add many more. Unfortunately, the deer also love the tasty roses. Maintaining a garden is bittersweet but a setback brings opportunity; I'm excited to procure my roses, plant and share the blessed blooms.

Every day, I marvel at my good fortune to have been able to make a life out of breeding roses. My greatest satisfaction is to see the pleasure my roses give to gardeners and rose lovers worldwide.

—David Austin

Both Ralph Moore and David Austin received the distinguished Officer of the British Empire (OBE) designation for their service to horticulture. They both enjoyed literature and published books on the subject of roses and poetry. Both men exemplify extraordinary tenacity by ignoring the naysayers and refusing to succumb to a succession of challenges. Both followed their passions and embodied the spirit to continue to create and innovate even when they thought God's work was done.

Ralph Moore and David Austin led a quiet cause to achieve and inspire through following their dream, not someone else's dream. They led the development of a commodity that didn't exist or improved upon one that did.

Lakeside Organics: "Get 'er done!"

In high school, Dick Peixot (pronounced Pichote) grew beans on a 55-acre farm in the Pajaro Valley on California's Central Coast. In 1996, those acres became the original site of Lakeside Organics, and, due to the growing demand for organic produce, Peixoto converted the entire 2,500-acre farm from traditional to organic farming within five years. Today, Lakeside Organics is the largest shipper-grower, family-owned organic farm in the United States. Peixoto sells 50-plus varieties of crops, all non-GMO, including an array of lettuces, root crops, Brussel sprouts, green beans, avocadoes, and is the only organic grower of Fioretto (a natural hybrid of the brassica family).

Peixoto lives by his mission to *grow certified organic*. He applies companion planting and introduces parasites and ladybugs to reduce aphid and pest populations. If unable to eradicate pests through natural means, the fields are plowed under; "a tough decision," according to Peixoto.

Hard work and his "Get 'er done" mantra defines Dick Peixoto, the son of a potato farmer and Portuguese immigrant. Even in his 24th year of operation, you will find Peixoto behind the wheel of his pick-up inspecting his crops daily. When Peixoto brought in consultants to advise him on how to better his business, they left scratching their heads saying, "Just keep doing what you're doing!"

> *We choose to work with Mother Nature to aid us in our troubles.*
> —Dick Peixoto

While it appears Peixoto has been on an upward trajectory since his youth, it couldn't be further from the truth. Peixoto admits to being broke twice since going organic. "Couldn't even charge for a burrito at Taco Bell," he said.[111] In 1977, owing $8,000 for fuel, the vendor cut off his credit—no fuel, no farm! An angel, in the form of a fuel vendor, not only extended credit but paid off his debt in exchange for future business—a *quid pro quo* that continues 40 years later.

Peixoto "pays it forward" in a big way contributing to more than 17 local charities, and donates over 300,000 tons of produce annually. Reflecting on his own financial challenges, Peixoto empathizes, "people experience circumstances beyond their control and need help." He contributed $2 million dollars to an agricultural learning center to educate the next generation of agrarians. According to Peixoto, "The learning center is about getting young people back on the farm and discovering agriculture as a viable modern career path."[112]

Following one's passion and tenacity through the tough times are the lessons Moore, Austin and Peixoto exemplify.

More Authentic Leaders

While Lee Iacocca begs the question in his book, *Where Have All The Leaders Gone?*,[113] I have come to admire a few business leaders for being genuine, and in doing so, led successful companies by putting their employees first.

In the early 1900s, Thomas J. Watson, Sr. became general manager of IBM. According to an anecdote told by Peter Drucker in the video, *Leading in a Time of Change*, at one point IBM was nearly bankrupt when Watson's wife encouraged him to get out of the house and attend a meeting of local business representatives. At the meeting he met a librarian who was looking for a solution to cataloguing books. After hearing Thomas Watson describe his calculating machines, she told Watson she wanted to purchase four of his calculators. Her order saved the company.[114]

Watson is responsible for creating a culture of "blue-suited," well-groomed salesman with a penchant for customer service. He targeted the mainframe business, as opposed to small business machines, and doubled earnings in the first year. Watson built the IBM image based upon a strategy of substantial sales incentives, excellence in customer support, company pride and staff loyalty. He, too, lived his core values of putting the customer first, and treating his staff with great respect, especially at a time when workers were seen as cogs in a machine. He hired the first disabled employee—at a time when many were institutionalized. He encouraged any employee to approach him with complaints, concerns or ideas. He introduced the "open-door policy," and led an organization that respected its employees when such access to executives was unheard of in business.

It's 1911 at a typical morning sales meeting at National Cash Register Company (NCR) where Watson, Sr. was CEO, and his staff "has nothing to offer" in the way of new ideas. Watson states, "The trouble with every one of you is that you don't think enough!" Carrying the idea to IBM, Watson coined the slogan, THINK, and the genesis of IBM's education department in 1916 began. The THINK slogan subsidized sports teams, family outings and a company band. Not only was Watson's THINK policy his mantra, but also his belief in work-life balance for his employees. The THINK motto leads the charge to this day and is incorporated in product lines such as the Thinkpad laptop.[115]

The HP Way

The founders of Hewlett Packard created a culture that mostly remains today. David Packard and Bill Hewlett knew their employees by name and it was not uncommon for both of these individuals to routinely take a seat with an employee to learn about them and their work. Hewlett and Packard were as close to the janitorial staff as the executive staff, and treated everyone equally. Their authentic approach to leadership was built on the philosophy and values of *walking around management*. They were not emulating other leaders, but modeling behavior as the architects of such. Hewlett and Packard (HP) are a case study in highly-effective leadership. The HP way was built on a foundation of family values, an unshakeable foundation of intrinsic ethics that leveled the playing field. At HP everyone was important—not just a select few.[116]

Made in America

Sam Walton, founder of Walmart and Sam's Club, is a notable leader and visionary. He started the movement of deep discounting and made low pricing his company's competitive advantage. He knew how to draw crowds and make shopping a fun experience for the customer and Walmart associates. He is the first to admit the company got off the ground due to the work ethic of his southern employees, and created a mission and culture based upon giving customers

In order to survive we need to keep changing the things we do... get to know your customers, let them see you on the [sales] floors doing whatever it takes to keep the store operating.

—Sam Walton

and associates what they wanted: *a wide assortment of good quality merchandise, the lowest possible prices, guaranteed satisfaction with what you buy; friendly, knowledgeable service, convenient hours, free parking and a pleasant shopping experience.* Despite jeers, he was determined to offer customers the lowest price, even if by just a penny.[117] Sam Walton was looked upon by some of the Wall Street folks as a bumpkin prior to going public. Who ultimately were the real rubes?

The Saturday morning meetings were part of the Walmart business culture. He demanded all managers to show up on Saturday for what was always a "surprise agenda." One of his managers said none of the team would miss these meetings even if they were not required. Sam Walton knew how to entertain and make business enjoyable, building a culture by spending time with his employees having fun!

In the vein of having fun, Sam Walton led by placing himself at the center of staff and customers, immersing himself in fact-finding and observing to best support employees and patrons. He continued to reinvent Walmart to maintain that competitive advantage of the lowest possible price. In order to survive we need to keep changing the things we do. Sam Walton flew his own airplane to scope out new sites for distribution centers; buying direct from the manufacturer and strategically placing distribution sites close to the stores translated to lower prices. He was a leader who lived his mission: *get to know your customers, let them see you on the [sales] floors doing whatever it takes to keep the store operating.*

It Was The Right Thing To Do

On December 11, 1995 Malden Mills Company burned down, leaving 3,000 employees out of work. Instead of taking the $300 million dollars insurance money and retiring, owner Aaron Feuerstein continued to pay his employees their regular salaries worth $25 million

You are not permitted to oppress the working man,
because he's poor and he's needy, amongst your brethren
and amongst the non-Jews in your community. I got a lot
of publicity...I don't think that speaks well for our times...
at the time in America of the greatest prosperity, the god of
money has taken over to an extreme.[118]

—Aaron Feuerstein

dollars. In a 1996 *Parade Magazine* article about the CEO, he said: *I have a responsibility to the worker, both blue-collar and white-collar. I have an equal responsibility to the community.* Feuerstein thought it *unconscionable* to destroy the cities of Lawrence and Methuen by putting 3,000 people out of work, and felt a duty to provide employment for so many. He spoke of his study of the Torah as the root for staying this ethical line. Feuerstein not only spent the $300 million dollars insurance money, but an additional $100 million dollars to update the plant to be worker and environmentally friendly. *I think it was a wise business decision, but that isn't why I did it. I did it because it was the right thing to do,* he said.[119]

True Purpose Beyond Profits

A case study in customer service is the Marriott Company. Willard Marriott Sr. started a rootbeer stand in 1927; that stand grew into the first Hot Shoppes Restaurant. Then he and his son, William Jr., grew the company into a global hotel brand of 3,700 hotels in 74 countries before William Marriott Jr., who worked 60 years for the company, turned over the reins at age 80 to Arne Sorensen, the first non-family member to be a CEO.[120]

William Marriott Sr. espoused a leadership philosophy that was unprecedented in his time. In the book, *Without Reservations*, William Jr. writes about the core values his father deeply believed and committed to embed in the corporate culture. His "purpose over profits" and to "put people first" was entrenched internally and aligned with every element of day-to-day customer service. He encouraged employees to continuously improve themselves and promoted individuals who sought to do so. He supported housekeepers to be the first to put their children through college, and was proud when an employee who started as a waiter became CEO 35 years later. Marriott Sr. was not only an advocate of his employees reinventing themselves but the entire company's success is never final. *Create conditions for good business success and you'll create good business success in the future.*

The Case Study in Doing the Right Thing

Almost 40 years later, the Tylenol case remains the classic example of "doing the right thing" under dire circumstances. In 1982, a murderous act was committed resulting in the deaths of seven individuals in the Chicago area—all deaths attributed to one deranged individual separating the two pieces of the capsule and mixing cyanide with the acetaminophen contents of a few Tylenol capsules. The Johnson & Johnson Company's chairman, James Burke, exemplified leadership that put customers before profit. Without equivocation, Burke ordered 31 million bottles immediately taken off the shelves anywhere Tylenol was sold. There was no deliberating the cost or the possibility of financial ruin to Johnson & Johnson. Such a recall was unprecedented.

Johnson & Johnson's (J & J) strategy after the recall was equally laudable. J & J offered coupons for free Tylenol and rebates for the same. Turning crisis into opportunity, tamperproof bottles and caplets were brought to market as a result. The caplet was ingenious and offered customers an option to the traditional capsule that had been opened and tainted with cyanide; an action no longer feasible with the solid caplet. Subsequent to this event, the FDA mandated tamperproof packaging. While J & J lost and invested millions of dollars, losing 30-plus percent of its market share in the analgesic market, it recovered as a result of the exemplary leadership throughout this terrorist attack. Any business leader can profess a code of ethics, yet acting it out when a company's solvency is at issue demonstrates prototypical leadership.[121]

First and foremost, put people first. We pursue excellence, act with integrity, embrace change and serve our world. Take good care of employees and they'll take good care of the customers, and they'll return again and again...[122]

—William Marriott Sr.

Your Employees Come First

On Bosses' Day, 16,000 of his employees took out a one-page ad in *USA Today* to honor the man whom they admired, Herb Kelleher, founder and CEO of Southwest Airlines. Herb Kelleher, who had a high regard for his mother, said, "My mother taught me that your employees come first. If you treat them well, then they treat the customers well, and that means your customers come back and your shareholders are happy." He believed all people were to be treated the same as he'd like to be treated, and lived out this belief over the course of his leadership. In negotiations, after asking the pilots to freeze their salary in exchange for Southwest options, he too froze his salary. His workers recalled, "He was able to remember all his employee's names, even if I only saw him once a year."

Body and Soul

Anita Roddick, the founder of The Body Shops, caught my attention in the 1990s when I read her autobiography, *Body and Soul*.[123] It would be hard to find a more authentic leader than Ms. Roddick, who founded an international company on the premise of refillable bottles of unscented body lotions made with all-natural products. Roddick saw through the high-margin perfume and cosmetic industry that made significant profits from packaging and alluring marketing. She described feeling like an *alien* when she attended workshops among the *big boys like Revlon and Estee Lauder. All I learned was how to be uncomfortable.*

What astounded me, even to this day, is the story of her expansion to a second store. After her first shop made a moderate success, Anita Roddick was determined to open a second shop. In 1976, banks wouldn't lend money to a woman with no collateral, and with her husband away, she chose to offer a 50 percent share of her business to

My mother taught me that your employees come first. If you treat them well, then they treat the customers well, and that means your customers come back and your shareholders are happy.

—Herb Kelleher, Southwest founder

Ian McGlinn, a friend's boyfriend, and owner of an auto mechanic shop. Roddick offered the exchange for the infusion of £4000 pounds. Even at the time of the 1991 writing of *Body and Soul*, the £4000 pounds turned into $141 million dollars. I couldn't imagine being comfortable giving away half of the hard work of what the Roddicks built; a business that grew 50 percent per year through the 90s and had a value in the billions of dollars. According to Roddick, *Giving away half the business is considered by many as the biggest mistake I have ever made, but I don't resent it. I needed the money. I needed it quickly and Ian was the only one then who would give it to me...50 percent stake in two small shops was hardly a fortune.*

Anita Roddick's passion for product purity didn't stop with refillable bottles. She led a number of campaigns promoting natural products and vehemently fought against animal testing, a drive to eradicate such testing in the cosmetic industry. In the early years, Roddick expanded her business making verbal deals with many women who came to her wanting to open one of her shops. A mutual agreement was made in that her product would be sold, and, in exchange, the business operation would be left in the hands of each location owner. Not knowing she was actually franchising, Roddick expanded her company into London's elite Covent Gardens and Portobello Road. By 1979, Body Shops opened in Athens and Sweden and Roddick was happy to share the wealth with many along the way.

I admire Anita Roddick not only for her business acumen but her innate belief that business needs to be part of a community: to give back, not just to take. Roddick again delivered on her inherent mission of contributing to the community you serve when she created a Department of Activism within her company whose mission called for every Body Shop to participate in its community: working with the elderly, the Red Cross, and giving facials to the underserved or sick.

To succeed you have to believe in something with such a passion that it becomes a reality.

—Anita Roddick

Roddick instituted the Red Letter System allowing anyone to go straight to the top to complain without repercussions, and opened its first Body Shop Day Care Center in 1990. Undaunted, and, despite her position of power, Roddick believed leadership should encourage its successors *not just to follow but, to overtake.*

Anita Roddick is an authentic entrepreneur in my eyes because she led the way in social conscience—not only demanding all her shops give back by *doing* for the local community, but giving back globally as well through Greenpeace, Amnesty International, sustaining the rainforests and the *Stop the Burning* campaign. Roddick actually employed an anthropologist to ensure entire societies/cultures would not be lost: *Losing the collected wisdom of the rainforest tribes would be like burning every library in the world without bothering to look at what was on the shelves,* she said. The Body Shop founder's core values were not based upon a popular trend but deep passion for sustainability and respect for the environment. According to Roddick, *along with the profit and loss sheets, I would want to know about the profit and loss for the environment, or the community or the third world.*

The "Reluctant Businessman"

An admitted "rebel of the corporate culture" who wrote that " politicians and businessmen were greaseballs and corporations the source of all evil," yet, Yvon Chouinard amassed a billion-dollar fortune as a businessman. *Let my people go surfing,* subtitled, *The Education of a Reluctant Businessman,* Chouinard begins his book by stating that he never dreamed of being a businessman, but his business career began as a young, innovative entrepreneur creating lightweight pitons out of scrap metal from an "old chrome-molybdenum steel blade of a harvester."[124] He used the pitons for his record-breaking Yosemite ascents and sold them for $1.50 to climbers who knew a good thing

Conventional retailers trained for a sale; we trained for knowledge. They trained with an eye on the balance sheet; we trained with an eye on the soul. Their basic business strategy was through kindness. Without a business education, the Body Shop was/is strictly driven by their own moral compass.

—Samantha Roddick
(Anita's daughter)

when they saw one. His next investment was in a drop forging die with money borrowed from his parents, adding lightweight carabiners to his menu of items sold out of the back of his car. All this business-making and still a teenager. Cruising the California coast surfing and selling, intermixed with climbing, Chouinard was a bit of a truant until drafted and honorably discharged from the military—despite his insufferable antics while in the service. After the 1964 first ascent up Yosemite's El Capitan's North American Wall, not only did Chouinard become a climbing icon, demand for his product exploded. His first shop, Chouinard Equipment Company, was opened in Ventura, California in 1970—the same year he married Malinda Pennoyer (still married 51 years later).

A 1970 visit to an old mill in England and the purchase of a rugby shirt in Scotland would be a turning point for Chouinard and the advent of what would become Patagonia—one of the largest manufacturers and retailers of outdoor equipment and sportswear worldwide.

Chouinard's story is fascinating at many levels but the most intriguing is how steadfast he has remained to his core values. He has incorporated his respect for nature, and all he has enjoyed of its beauty, into every element of his company. He insists that Patagonia locations are created from existing buildings using refurbished materials, as was done to rehabilitate his second store, and Chouinard's favorite, in San Francisco's North Beach area.

Chouinard's deep commitment to his core values extend to his employees, suppliers and contractors. He makes no concessions when it comes to quality. Chouinard has maintained an environment of flextime for staff, among other benefits. Again, in keeping with of his core values, Chouinard insisted his employees be paid during the COVID-19 pandemic.[125]

We are a part of nature and as we destroy nature we destroy ourselves. It's a selfish thing to want to protect nature.

—Yvon Chouinard

Giving back, he started the 1 percent for the Planet organization donating one percent of Patagonia's gross sales to grassroots organizations who have made it their mission to protect the environment.

Our Primary Objective Is to Please the Customer

Paul Orfalea had difficulty reading as a child in the 1940s—a typical report card filled with Cs and Ds—and says he was grateful for his mother's persistence to find him help. Orfalea is a self-described dyslexic with ADHD who appreciates the support of his parents and friends who helped him to overcome his barriers to learning.

> *Orfalea said his lineage of entrepreneurs encouraged him to start a business versus get a job. Entrepreneurship is not about owning a business, it's about owning your life.*

His keen observation of the money students spent at bookstore copiers inspired him to open his first copy center near a university. Thus, Kinko's was born and the rest is history. Paul Orfalea is an inspiration to entrepreneurs beyond his tenacity and astute business acumen because of how he integrated his core values into Kinko's foundation and leadership style. His core principles are reflected in how he built and led Kinko's. He turned his shortcomings into strengths as a leader.

Orfalea believes *"Our coworkers are the foundation of our success."* Employees consider themselves part of the Kinko's family. *We trust and care for each other, and treat everyone with respect.* Orfalea believes in giving the people what they want...by building both recognition and opportunity into your company's value system, you can share plenty of glory and 'money' with the coworkers who desire these things—no matter what, thank your coworkers.[126]

I felt blessed with the inability to sit still, as the restlessness got me out into my stores...Too many executives manage by spreadsheets alone...you've got to be out in the world looking for obstacles to remove and new opportunities to exploit.

—Paul Orfalea

Paul Orfalea confirmed what I learned over a period of years studying leaders of every sector when he documented that *an executive
needs time to reflect.*

---

*Whenever I felt down, whenever I started wondering what
homeless shelter I would die in, [my mother] would buck me
up by telling me: you know, Paul, the A students work for the B
students, the C students run the companies and the D students
dedicate the buildings.*

*In company cultures that embrace the inevitability of change,
innovation becomes habitual rather than crisis-driven; the
business adapts organically to its changing environment.
Routine is fine in a world that doesn't change.*[127]

—Paul Orfalea

I believe authentic leadership is innate and not taught, despite
some documented thought to the contrary. Just as no one could
tell Mother Teresa, Martin Luther King, Jr., or Nelson Mandela to
find a cause or be given a task to perform, their passion arose from
within— intrinsically, and from an ethical platform no one else could
build for them. Gandhi was not a hired negotiator, but a crusader
who changed history because he was willing to devote his life to a
deeply-rooted passion for freedom from British rule.

I am not the only one who believes authentic leadership translates
to better overall outcomes. According to an article in the *Academy
of Management*, "Taking Stock of Moral Approaches to Leadership: An Integrative Approach to Ethical, Authentic and Servant
Leadership," authors G. James Lemoine, et al, discuss the results
of an extensive literature review. The authors conclude that there is

a correlation between moral leadership and positive outcomes for both the organization and employee.[128] While we tend to negate the importance of the character of leader and the success of an organization, the literature states otherwise.

Robert Greenleaf, an individual whom I greatly admire and studied at length during my doctoral studies, was a subscribing member of his servant leadership organization for years. His philosophy was always included in my courses on leadership. Greenleaf rose through the ranks as an engineer at AT&T, and, during his 38-year tenure, was influential in hiring the first women and Blacks into more prestigious positions. In 1970, Robert Greenleaf published an essay "The Servant as Leader" in which he distinguishes between an individual who seeks to be a leader first as opposed to being a servant first and leader second.[129]

In a November 2019 Forbes article, Scott Kriens, co-founder and past CEO of Juniper Networks, discussed a sentinel moment after his father's death that led him to question his "real purpose in life, despite having achieved monetary and business success."[130] While it appears Kriens was learning later in life the need to set aside time for reflection, he now meditates regularly and has provided a place of refuge and personal growth for leaders. In 2017, Scott Kriens and his wife, Joanie, opened the 1440 Foundation, subsequently the 1440 Multiversity, in Scotts Valley, California. The 75-acre campus, with a conference center and space to eat and sleep amid the redwoods, was named after Joanie Kriens inspiration to divide a 24-hour day into minutes.

I believe there was a reason why I came across the story of Scott and Joanie Kriens while doing research for my book. There are a plethora of leaders in the Silicon Valley but the story of their philanthropy, and especially Joanie Kriens "moment of mindfulness" while working in her garden compelled me to look further into their story. You see, much of the content in my book has come from those moments of mindfulness that come from somewhere else—an inspiration that was forwarded to me. Joanie Kriens and many of us find such revelations in the quiet splendor of our gardens and nature. Where do you find such moments of creativity? You have to make the time and space for such insight.

Reflect in Your Garden

Does a leader make the organization or does the organization make the leader?

Who are the authentic leaders you admire? Why?

Make a list of qualities you believe make an effective leader.

Make a list of qualities you believe make a leader authentic.

Make a list of your leadership qualities.

Do you consider yourself to be an authentic leader? Why?

How will you know if you are an effective leader?

Identify at least one individual you consider a servant leader. Do you consider yourself a servant leader? If so, why?

How much time do you set aside for reflection?

Culture

As discussed earlier, organizational theory encompasses organizational design, development and behavior. In the hierarchy of organizational theory, the culture of an organization is classified under both the design and behavior within an organization and overlaps communication, leadership and group dynamics. Keep in mind that an organization is not limited to a business or company but any group of individuals with a shared purpose: a family, society, association, church, school, or similar entities are considered an organization each with its own culture.

Culture, typically defined as a set of goals, shared attitudes, values and practices that characterize an institution, or organization, is one of the most difficult concepts to understand. An organization, as referred to here, is a compilation of systems, and, in nature, as in business, systems are made up of interdependent parts. The flow between and among the parts will determine success, or barriers to such. This flow begins with a design, but is executed through an environment that encourages open communication. In turn, the only way a leader or owner can create such a culture is through an acute understanding of the interrelationship of all the organization's parts.

We all use the term *cultural differences*, and seem to have an immediate understanding of what that means. However, what we are really referring to are symbols of a culture: how we communicate, dress code, what is acceptable behavior, the hierarchy of communication (sometimes referred to as chain of command), how free-flowing communication and decision-making exists among its members. A business's culture is not only observed, but discerned perusing its policy and procedure manuals, mission and vision statements, organizational chart and by interviewing staff. Edgar Schein is the preeminent authority on the subject of culture. His description of culture includes: observed behavior and common language, group

Culture of a group is defined as a pattern of shared basic assumptions that the group learned as it solved its problems of external adaptation and internal integration, that has worked well enough to be considered valid and, therefore, to be taught to new members as the correct way to perceive, think and feel in relation to those problems.[131]

—Edgar Schein

norms, espoused values, philosophy, rules of the game, embedded skills, climate, mental models, shared meanings, artifacts and symbols.[132]

A business's culture becomes tangible to the consumer in the symbols or expectations we begin to conjure as we imagine entering one of its establishments. For example, the symbol of the golden arches or any logo summons anticipation: going to McDonald's we expect a certain menu, service and predictable layout. Imagine going to Costco versus Safeway or Kroger versus 7-11; think of Nordstrom versus Marshalls and Walmart, each with its own distinct culture. Amazon versus…well then there's Amazon in a class of its own.

Within a well-led organization every department and team should reflect the vision and mission of the organization. Have you ever left a business saying to yourself, *This is the last time I'll ever come here again* or vice versa, *I'll bring my business to this merchant whenever possible*? Despite this alignment of vision and mission among departments and teams, each create their own culture developed over time. To some degree we self-select the type of culture where we choose to work. For example, the inner-city emergency departments I chose to work had a culture different from community hospital emergency departments. Within any emergency department the three shifts, typically, day, afternoon and nights, each had its own personality and behavior. At times, such subcultures can have conflicting views with the macro organization but often are set aside when confronted with a negative outside influence. As an accountant you may choose to work for a hospital chain, university, large church, agricultural business, in retail or technology—a large partnership of accountants or small nonprofit. The cultures will differ, as you may expect, each recognizable by its core values, policies, logos, artifacts of founders, and more.

Walt Disney created a culture that remained the same until his death. Sam Walton, Walmart and Sam's Club founder, and Ray Kroc, developer of McDonalds, each one a notable leader, created a culture we all recognize by the flow of the store, menu, price of its goods and cleanliness of facilities; the culture did not create the leader, they created the culture.

Culture is shaped over time and is difficult to change. Hewlett Packard has long been revered as the case study in *avant-garde* leadership that respected all employees for their contribution to the organization. David Packard and John Hewlett led as they espoused, with integrity and sincere care for their human resources—they lived their core values. In an article, "The HP Ways: A Lesson on Strategy and Culture,"[133] the author chronicles the many iterations of its leaders and each one's attempt to create a successful, transformational change while maintaining the embedded culture. Once again, I pose to you: Does an organization create the culture, or the culture create an organization?

We hate change, yet it happens at record speeds. Adapt or die. In order to be competitive in the 21st century market, businesses need to erase and replace their cultural capital. For instance, companies have moved from long-term to contract help for work on projects. William Bridges predicted this in his 1994 book *Job Shift: How to Prosper in a World Without Jobs*. In early 2021, an estimated 57.3 million freelance workers are part of the gig or project-based U.S. workforce.[134] An August 18, 2018 article in *Forbes* states, 57 million workers, or 36 percent, are part of the gig economy; Uber, Door Dash, Etsy, Amazon, Ebay and other e-businesses are part-time employment for many in between jobs or looking for temporary work. An Intuit 2020 study predicted that 80 percent of large companies will utilize a workforce that engage on a contract or project basis.[135] Such names as "flexible workforce," "gig" workers (coined after musicians), or independent contractors are terms describing this group of emerging workers that is growing for a variety of reasons: lack of loyalty between employers and employees, technology-promoting mobility, costs of benefits, seeking work-life balance, and a growing desire to be more in control of work choices.

Harvard Business Review published the results of a study in their March-April, 2018 issue, "Thriving in the Gig Economy." The article addresses the ever-present need for community even among the independent workforce, a home or familiar self-created workplace that one yearns to be in, surrounded by a fully-equipped environment to work. Self-described, this freelance workforce admits to learning about themselves—their purpose. They visualize a better sense of themselves as they grapple with the uncertainly that comes with this independent lifestyle, particularly the uncertainty of the source of their next paycheck.

Reflect in Your Garden

What kind of business culture do you want to create?

Is the culture at home the one you wanted for yourself and your family?

Describe the lingering sense your friends would feel after being at your home and the culture they experienced being with your family.

Does a leader create the culture or the culture choose the leader?

Identify the symbols that distinguish the culture of your business. How do the policies and procedures, and mode of communication, reflect your business' culture?

What Does An Unprecedented Merger Have To Do With Culture?

I had the privilege of writing a case study with one of my graduate nursing students employed at Stanford Medical Center. The case centered around an unprecedented merger between two stellar, world-renowned teaching medical centers located on the Central Coast of California: Stanford Medical Center and the University of California San Francisco (UCSF) Medical Center, that included Mt. Zion Hospital.[136] The 1997 merger was an exceptional teaching case because it covered all elements of a business organization: finance, economics, leadership, information systems, group dynamics and culture. I was afforded the opportunity to interview the chief executive officer (CEO) of the newly-merged, UCSF Stanford Health Center, Peter Van Etten, as well as the chief financial officer (CFO), on two separate occasions. I garnered sage lessons from those interviews that I've shared with many students of business and nursing leadership.

The merger was championed by individuals who left the organizations prior to the union of these two very different organizational models, and, as expected, the most prominent consulting firms were part of the planning. Formulating this amalgamation of two disparate organizations took longer to meld than the union lasted.[137] After two years of marital discord, the de-merger was announced in 1999 on the very day I interviewed the CFO! Upon entering our meeting, he announced he had just come from the meeting that sealed the vote to de-merge. With chalk in hand, he chronicled the reasons why the two medical centers could no longer coexist. Despite the vows of "what's yours is mine and mine is yours," daily life didn't accept the financial terms under such conciliatory harmony. Stanford Medical Center is a nonprofit, private institution as opposed to UCSF's public teaching facility. UCSF Medical Center had a rather arcane information system, versus Stanford's more advanced enterprise-wide system. Most importantly, a need to meld the patient databases was necessary. Despite the existing information systems, an overarching system representing the two medical centers' patients, plus Mt. Zion Hospital and Julia Packard Children's Hospital patients, all needed to be coalesced into a single, costly, database. Additionally, how do you fuse labor union workers from a public institution with several other labor unions, including a private nursing union, with a national nurses' union?[138]

Reimbursement for patient care was plummeting during the growth years of managed care, while demand for access was on the incline. In the first year of the merger, the newly formed organization saw a savings of $11 million dollars, most of which came from staff reductions. However, in the second year, the UCSF Stanford Health System lost $20 million dollars. In an August 5, 1999 meeting, Stanford Medical Center's chief operating officer, Malinda Mitchell, highlighted the fact that "the two organizations entered the merger as equals...things have changed." UCSF's losses due to Mt. Zion Hospital, as of 1999 fiscal year-end, were $56 million versus Stanford's $6 million.[139] I was told in a rather poignant interview that Mt. Zion Hospital should have been closed, but because the hospital served a significant public need, such a decision was difficult to make. However, according to the chief operating officer, the next year's projections showed a breakeven between both organizations: $20 million loss for UCSF and $20 million gain for Stanford. The vow of richer or poorer was omitted from the treatise melding these two organizations. In a 1999 *Health Affairs* article penned by Peter Van Etten, "Camelot or Common Sense? The Logic Behind the UCSF/Stanford Merger," Van Etten attributes one cause of the failed merger to the fact that each academic medical center is different and should not depend on "conventional wisdom" to dictate a one-size-fits-all strategy.[140]

While financial woes seemed to signal the final blow, I believe the real cause of death was an incongruent culture between dissimilar institutions. The merged entities were dealing with physician faculty and medical staff at both facilities carved out of the top tier of physicians nationwide—a confluence of experts from both organizations. These physician specialists had garnered a corner of the medical world open to few. Was this arrangement synergistic or one of noncooperation? An ongoing source of conflict was the ever-present question as to "whose home are we visiting today?" The mere 33 miles that separated the two institutions could be an hour-plus drive in the traffic-congested Bay Area. A routine meeting, otherwise held in the onsite conference room, now became a half-day affair.

I learned that physician faculty were not well represented in the formulating stages of the merger—a big mistake. Leadership and Consulting 101 teaches you to bring all the stakeholders to the planning table. In a nutshell, it is my belief the biggest contributor to the downfall of the blended family of superior medical centers was the failure to recognize the significance of the cultural differences between the two organizations.

The cultural differences were not limited to the physicians. How do you formulate an organizational chart that supplants one of the leaders who held the number one position into second place? Such was the case when William Kerr, a 19-year veteran at UCSF and CEO, became executive vice-president (EVP) and chief operating officer (COO) of the newly-formed organization. This shifting of places on the organizational chart was not limited to the C-suite and included management of nurses and ancillary departments such as laboratory, pharmacy and radiology.[141]

An interesting epilogue is the fact the two medical centers co-mingled their students and faculty to staff the San Francisco Hospital in the 19th century until a 1953 decision was made to relocate Stanford

Medical Research Center down the peninsula from San Francisco to Palo Alto. The vacated facility that once housed Stanford Medical Center became the new home for Stanford physicians who didn't want to move to Palo Alto, and today is California Presbyterian Medical Center (CPMC).[142] This August 11, 1999 article in the Stanford Report reads like an obituary:

> *UCSF Stanford Health Care announced Monday, August 9, that Peter Van Etten, president and chief executive officer, and William Kerr, executive vice president and chief operating officer, will resign from their positions, effective August 16....praise [for] Van Etten and Kerr for their contributions and service.[143] On behalf of our board, I want to thank both Peter and Bill for the many years of outstanding leadership they have provided in their previous roles at the UCSF and Stanford hospitals and to UCSF Stanford Health Care.[144]*

The interim consultant team performed their duty: on November 24, 1999, Mt. Zion's emergency department and inpatient units ceased operations.[145]

Family Business and Culture

My father was an entrepreneur who built two small businesses. In the 1960s, he began investing in single-family homes to "fix-up" and rent. Over the next 50 years the real estate amassed into multiple-residential and commercial building assets. My mother, too, became involved in the early years, collecting rents, showing apartments and bookkeeping. I confess to starting in real estate at age 12, answering calls for rentals and going with mom to clean and collect rents. At 60 years old, dad went into the furniture rental business, the only one of its kind in our area. Over the years, siblings moved in and out of working relationships with my dad.

The culture of a small family built and operated business is emblematic of the family values, and should infiltrate every element of the business. The transfer of power to a son or daughter may prove too difficult of a shift from being the patriarch; respect of an outsider's opinion over a son's or daughter's is fast-track to conflict.

Until age and ill-health challenged my father to manage the business, he held the reins tight. My two brothers and I, out of six siblings, became heavily involved in business operations until years after my parents passed. Our accountant commented, "Among the siblings, you will never reach 'fairness or equity' as the business is dissolved." How right she was, and, without all partners sharing the same goals and vision, the end result is conflict.

My father never thought about succession planning, which is not uncommon in family businesses when family members have not been involved until the elder owner retires. Until my father was physically unable to work the long hours he was accustomed to, even at age 87, he fought to maintain complete control over all aspects of the business. Effective leaders know how to delegate in order to oversee the "big picture" versus micromanaging.

When multiple siblings are a factor, there is a sense of entitlement among those who have not been involved with regard to equal control and decision-making, as well as compensation. Such asymmetry of core values leads to the demise of the company.

Culture and Do Unto Others

One final note on the subject of culture: Another approach to "adapt or die," is to place yourself in the shoes and world of the individual attempting to adapt to a new environment; to learn about their culture as a way of easing their transition. In this manner, you are both learning about each other, and, in doing so, each evolving. For example, we've all welcomed a new business associate, team member or new neighbor. Should the new person be expected to assimilate to thrive and earn our friendship, or could we ask the newcomer, "What can we learn about you in order to help you adjust to your new life here?"

> *Great leaders love to see people grow. The day you are afraid of them being better than you is the day you fail as a leader.*
>
> —Jack Welch

GROUP DYNAMICS

To reiterate, the elements of organizational behavior are leadership, culture and group dynamics. Group dynamics is further broken down into all methods of communication within and external to the organization.

COMMUNICATION

I can say without equivocation that the root cause of virtually every problem I was engaged to resolve in my consulting practice was a result of poor communication or miscommunication. Medical errors are often traced back to communication, and in the following scenario the world was riveted watching one of the century's greatest disasters unfold—the result of poor communication.

It was January 27, 1986, hours after the Challenger space shuttle launch had been scrubbed yet again. NASA leadership and ten Morton Thiokal engineers were assembled for a phone conference to discuss the next day's launch. Morton Thiokal was the engineering firm contracted by NASA to design the Challenger's rocket booster. In the early evening teleconference, Morton Thiokal engineers in Utah presented data to NASA employees in Florida, indicating the

O-rings had not been tested at the low temperatures predicted for the next morning's launch. Consequently, Thiokol engineers recommended not to launch—an unprecedented event. NASA rocket booster manager, Larry Malloy, was "appalled" that Thiokol would present this information the night before launch.

> *I can say without equivocation that the root cause of virtually every problem I was engaged to resolve in my consulting practice was a result of poor communication or miscommunication.*

In a memo to managers at Thiokol, one of NASA's booster rocket engineers, Roger Boisjoly, predicted six months before the Challenger launch that it would be "a catastrophe of the highest order" involving "loss of human life," should the Challenger launch at the low temperatures predicted. It was later learned this memo was never seen by anyone at NASA. Boisjoly spoke openly for decades after the disaster that he *would never consider it an accident.* The Challenger should have never left the ground according to Bob Ebeling, NASA engineer.

Returning to the night before launch, Larry Malloy of NASA prompted Joe Kilminster, vice president of Thiokal, to *take off your engineer hat and put on your management hat* and make a written decision to launch. Larry Malloy pushed Kilminster, to put pressure on Thiokal's engineers to stand behind their data or "make a decision to launch."

Pre-launch, NASA was under tremendous pressure after scrubbing the mission multiple times. The media was even suggesting that Teresa McAuliffe, the teacher-in-residence, would have to teach to empty classrooms on the weekend, should the launch be delayed again. The fact that one of the engineers was not present at the pre-launch meeting as well as the physical distance between participants (in Utah, Alabama and Florida) exacerbated the chaos.

After the disaster, President Reagan called for an investigation. The committee consisted of members including Charles Yeager, former astronauts Sally Ride and Neil Armstrong; Larry Malloy presented the engineers' data before the committee. The alarming moment came when Thiokal engineer Alan McDonald interrupted Larry Malloy to recount to the committee what really happened. He stated that the night before the liftoff Thiokal's engineers made a *no launch recommendation*. McDonald said later that he believed what was most heinous was NASA and Morton Thiokal trying to cover up what actually happened. In reality, there wasn't enough data to go ahead with the launch and the engineers were concerned because tests had not been run at the low temperatures expected at the early morning launch. McDonald advises young engineers to question recommendations *based on not what you know but what you don't know.*

The events leading up to the Challenger disaster have been laid out before the public so we will all continue to learn. In the following section, the pre-launch events are further scrutinized.[146]

The telling details chronicle the communication between all parties leading up to the launch.

The take-away: Do not be afraid to question nor be shamed into conformity of thought.

Groupthink

Under situations of extreme pressure, Groupthink, a phenomenon coined by Yale research psychologist Irving Janis, can drastically impact group decision-making. After dissecting the causative events of the Challenger accident, all the symptoms of Groupthink were at play—culminating in tragedy. Let's break down the symptoms of Groupthink using the events leading up to the Challenger disaster. First, Malloy emphasized how many times Roger Boisjoly was called a "complainer" and rebuffed by George Hardy, a NASA manager and lead on the Challenger launch. Boisjoly was put down for being overly sensitive and ostracized for thinking he was the only one concerned about doing the right thing. These are examples of the "out-group stereotypes" and a belief in the "inherent morality of the group." Hardy was quoted as saying, *"My God, do you want me to delay the launch until April? I am appalled that Thiokal would suggest not to launch the night before."* His disgust created "self-censorship and direct pressure on dissenters," giving an "illusion of unanimity" when asking the engineers why they did not object before when temperatures were also cold. Keep in mind memos of concern presented by Boisjoly were destroyed by his superiors who considered him a worrier and complainer; these individuals were considered "self-appointed mind guards" and symptomatic of Groupthink. Malloy repeatedly requested data from Thiokal engineers demonstrating that the O-rings would fail, but he was told such data did not exist since testing at the lower temperatures hadn't been performed. Malloy created uncertainty by suggesting that, *if the data didn't exist, the facts were inconclusive*—inferring the data was irrelevant; such plotting created a sense of "collective rationalization." The statement, *we've tested 24 or more times* led to the "sense of invulnerability." The idea that Thiokal engineers would question NASA's objectives gave rise to condemnations of the engineers as being of a "higher moral ground."[147]

Symptoms of Groupthink

1. Belief in the inherent morality of the group

2. Out-group stereotypes

3. Putting pressure on dissenters

4. Self-censorship

5. Illusion of unanimity

6. Collective rationalization

7. Sense of invulnerability

8. Emergence of self-appointed mind guards

In the writing of this book as I approached the topic of poor communication leading to deleterious effects, I, unfortunately, could have chronicled case after case in healthcare that led to near death or deleterious outcomes due to a failure to effectively communicate. Ignoring data or neglecting to uncover essential facts, have led to medical errors. Thanks to a plethora of clinicians who perform retrospective and root cause analyses and those that continuously improve systems designs, we are improving healthcare outcomes. The surgeon, Atul Gawande, embedded the simple use of checklists into medical processes and procedures so as to avoid medical oversights and errors.[148]

We learn from mistakes however egregious. Creating an environment that encourages open communication, without admonishment when mistakes do occur, lays a foundation for learning. More importantly,

Don't let us forget that the causes of our human actions are usually immeasurably more complex than our subsequent explanations of them.

—Dostoevsky

enlisting every employee to be acutely alert to the signs of an impending disaster empowers them to abort the actions before the error occurs. Let's look at one methodology used in risk mitigation.

Failure Mode Effects Analysis (FMEA)

Failure mode effects analysis (FMEA) was developed in the 1950s by reliability engineers, a subspecialty of systems engineers, to test every element of a system for potential failures. This methodology has been adopted by many other disciplines as a pre-or post-methodology investigative process to get to the root cause of a problem/systems failure. In healthcare the Institutes of Health (IHI) and Institute of Medicine (IOM) have developed a database of teaching cases in which the FMEA process has been used across all medical fields to prevent medical errors. The National Highway Traffic Safety Institute (NHTSA) uses the FMEA process to reconstruct the events of an accident— like the pieces of a puzzle chronicling the actions leading up to the accident, during the accident, and after the accident.[149]

Information is often ignored even when presented. This was not the case in the post analysis of the Challenger disaster, but the "lack of data" that caused a decision with such a deleterious outcome. Unfortunately, 17 years later, a second NASA disaster caused the deaths of the seven Columbia astronauts. The culture and processes within the systems at NASA were acutely scrutinized and in some ways NASA has never recovered.

In the quote below, please note the inclusion of the terms culture, systems and values, all topics discussed in this book.

> *There is just no question that is one of their primary*
> *observations, that what we need to do, we need to be focused*
> *on, is to examine those cultural procedures, those systems,*
> *the way we do business, the principles and the values that*
> *we adhere to as a means to improve and constantly upgrade*
> *to focus on safety objectives as well as the larger task before*
> *us of exploring and discovering on behalf of the American*
> *people.*[150]

NASA Facts NASA Press Conference on the Space Shuttle
Columbia
Sean O'Keefe, Administrator
Wednesday, August 27, 2003, 11:02 a.m.

As a nurse I never performed a task I did not feel comfortable carrying out, nor administer a drug that I felt was beyond my license to administer. As the president of Emergency Specialist Corporation, I recommended nurse contractors refuse to carry out a questionable order, or if he/she felt unsafe performing a task. My advice reminded the nurses that no one else would be on the witness stand testifying with them.

As I mentioned above, encouraging a culture of open communication not only reduces mistakes but encourages learning and innovation.

Organizational Learning

My favorite organizational theorist, Chris Argyris, Harvard Professor of Education and Organizational Behavior, contributed a great deal of research on the dysfunctions within organizations. Argyris introduced methodology to correct poor communication and, in doing so, opened the doors to enterprise-wide learning and change. In his book, *Overcoming Organizational Defenses: Facilitating Organizational Learning*,[151] Chris Argyris identifies seven "worldwide crucial errors" collected from managers.

First, *actions intended to increase understanding and trust often produce misunderstanding and mistrust.* Imagine an executive delegated an important task to her managers with clear expectations and deliverables. However, the managers failed to produce expected results because of their inability to communicate effectively among themselves. The executive is angered and disappointed, as well as upset at the absence of being brought up to date. Now the executive doesn't trust her reports and the managers go deeper underground; they refuse to, as Argyris says, "discuss the undiscussable"—to ask questions!

Second, *blaming others or the system for poor decisions.* This defensive behavior is probably the one most recognized by the reader. We have all witnessed a failure to take the deep dive into the truth. Protect the organization at all costs because the truth would cause shame and embarrassment, exposing proprietary information and a product recall—the result of a vendor's defective part.

Third, *organizational inertia.* Change is forever suspended because of the infinite excuses among staff. The list of reasons for resistance becomes long and pervasive. The adage "we've done it this way for years...we can't force staff to change...why fix something that is not broken...the staff will feel threatened." In his book, *Managerial*

Courage, Harvey Hornstein, describes such resistance as "idea killers." Hornstein states "[When] in doubt, do what you did yesterday. If it isn't working, do it twice as hard, twice as fast and twice as carefully." Peter Drucker states, "There is nothing quite so useless as doing with great efficiency something that should not be done at all."[152] The organization needs a strong team of champions who remain part of the change process until it's embedded in the culture.

Fourth, *upward communications for difficult issues are often lacking.* Argyris describes the feedback from line-level or mid-level staff disappearing into the "Bermuda triangle." According to Argyris, "Managers in the triangle have neither the respect for the rank and file nor an understanding of how better knowledge can enhance quality, output and efficiency." I, too, have witnessed critical information being suppressed not by middle management but a CEO to his board. He withheld the results of a vote of an influential executive committee when the outcome of the vote didn't fit the goals of the larger organization. In fact, the CEO was to receive a significant bonus for ensuring the goals of the macro organization were carried out—at any cost. This is not leadership but being a good soldier carrying out the real leader's agenda.

Fifth, *budget games are necessary evils.* Argyris describes some of the budget "games" as: *divide and conquer, it can't be measured.* Two favorite games are, *razzle-dazzle,* and *our program is priceless* in which you present so much data you confuse the recipient, and preach the idea that no amount of money should be an issue when it comes to saving human lives.

Sixth, *people do not behave reasonably, even when it is in their best interest.* Argyris identifies two of these games as: *paralysis by analysis* and *what the boss doesn't know won't hurt him.* He also includes such management errors: stalling, sabotage, strategic ineffectiveness, and indecision as self-destructive techniques.

Seventh, *the management team is often a myth*. According to Argyris, despite millions of dollars spent on team building, the reality is that *there is no management team…* it's a fable. Argyris goes so far as to state that all organizations suffer from organizational fancy footwork, defensive routines, and skilled incompetence. Unfortunately, such behavior is ubiquitous and why organizational change is so difficult.

In my work I've witnessed executives who are not leaders but good soldiers carrying out the wishes of those at the corporate level—top executives of a vertically integrated organization—rewarded for following orders and stifling objections. For example, community hospitals were in the business of serving the needs of their community. Today, these entities are part of a chain of hospitals likely headquartered in another state and serving the greater goals of the macro organization. Ideal communication breaks down all boundaries, opening the doors to ideas or concerns without censorship. Argyris proposes that most good ideas or concerns are squelched before ever getting to a higher level of the organization.

I have observed that line-level staff are aware of organizational dysfunctions and even provide a solution. However, due to centralized decision making and being intimidated to make recommendations, change is thwarted. As a consultant I was in a position to gather information from employees with whom I often felt held the answers to many of the problems in a company but were never given the authority to effect the change. For example, an employee came to me stating that a doctor who had a 9:00 a.m. patient would come to work exactly at 9:00 a.m. and subsequently fell behind the rest of the day. Everyone knew that the doctor's lack of timeliness was the problem, yet no one suggested a solution or felt empowered to address the issue until I, as the consultant, asked the questions. This is what Argyris calls "discussing the undiscussable." Frustration grew as the excessive wait times impacted all members of the staff who quelled patient complaints, and were held over at lunch and at the end of the day due to schedule delays. I brought all doctors and staff together for an open discussion and solutions to this problem. Not only did the staff feel empowered to expose the issues but were given the opportunity to participate in the change process. We tend to keep patching up a long-standing problem versus finding a solution that eradicates *the root* of the problem.

One method to ascertaining the root cause of a problem is utilizing "The Five Whys Method," the process of repeatedly asking "why" when a rationale is proposed. Respondents must be comfortable knowing their answers are not going to be censored. One must ask "why" at least *five times* to identify the root cause of the issue. Unfortunately, evoking that fourth or fifth response without edification is rare. I find getting too close to a cause creates an uncomfortable situation. In order to protect their positional power, managers often suppress what everyone needs to say and hear. According to Chris Argyris, for the sake of "morale" and "considerateness," they deprive employees and themselves of the opportunity to take responsibility for their own behavior by learning to understand it.

Nurses are given accolades for their ability to "work around" a situation, rather than undertake the investigatory process to query "why do we do things a certain way?" A nurse is applauded for finding a quick-fix solution that challenges proper protocol—throwing a solution at the "effect" versus drilling down to the root cause. Let's look at a common example of nurses responding in a single-loop manner. In this scenario medical equipment alarms signal an alert to the nursing staff that attention is needed to change an IV, administer medication or various other patient care tasks. To protect the patient's safety, their armband is synched to a barcoded device to ensure the patient's identity before the medication is released. Medication errors have been repeatedly documented due to the failure of the nurse to respond to an alarm, even cutting off the armband to abort the alarm. "Alarm fatigue" is the name given to the cause of such errors. I consider this ineptitude. Why would a nurse administer incorrect medication rather than challenge the alarm sensitivity? Today, numerous protocols have been put into place to perform a root cause analysis on such errors, however, does the nurse/employee feel comfortable admitting to averting or causing a mistake?

Double-loop learning depends on questioning the accepted way of doing things versus accepting what has been the norm for a long period of time. Throughout my consulting career I, too, observed that people resist change unless they have been engaged in the solution. In other words, if the individuals with whom the change is enacted upon are asked to participate in an uncensored session of breakthrough thinking toward finding a solution (all ideas are considered without comment), the same individuals feel empowered, and are more likely to follow through to sustain the change if given authority to do so.

W. Edwards Deming, an engineer, who is responsible for the quality movement post WWII Japan, later adopted in the U.S., devised the plan, do, study, act (PDSA) cycle. I witnessed many organizations jump on this bandwagon, only to abort the process when it came to the "study" part of the cycle.[153]

Effective communication overlaps all areas of organizational behavior and design. Absolutely no system-wide change is feasible without good communication. Max DePree states, "Good communication liberates us to do our jobs better. It is as simple as that." I do not believe you can be a successful leader without the ability to communicate effectively with those who work in your organization. Anita Roddick believes you must communicate the organization's purpose with a passion or "you may as well not be present." I mentioned earlier that performance goals should be aligned with the vision and

Talking can transform minds, that can transform behaviors which can transform institutions.

—Sheryl Sandberg

mission of the organization. Also, I cannot emphasize enough that leaders must listen to what people have to say about how they and the company is performing, including internal and external customers. I am encouraged by today's leaders such as Sheryl Sandberg, COO of Facebook, who embraces being forthright in your thoughts. She states in her book, *Lean In,* that, "Talking can transform minds, that can transform behaviors which can transform institutions."[154]

A student came to class week after week complaining about the multiple deficiencies at his workplace. His complaints spilled into every comment or activity in which he participated while in the classroom. After weeks of listening, I used the situation as a teaching/learning experience for everyone. I commented, *at some point when we choose to stay in a bad situation, we have to ask ourselves if we aren't part of the problem. Why do we continue to complain and choose inaction over action?* I was pleasantly surprised to hear that at the end of the course this student announced he'd found a new job. He began to question why he was so unhappy, thought he was stuck at his job, but found a way to make the transition he was *in fear of making.*

> *At some point when we choose to stay in a bad situation, we have to ask ourselves if we aren't part of the problem. Why do we continue to complain and choose inaction over action?*

TEAMS AND TEAM BUILDING

Due to the exceedingly rapid need to reinvent products requiring quick, agile decision-making, organizations assemble teams of individuals from multiple business functions to work on a project basis. A truly high-performing team of talented staff pulled from a variety of functional areas such as design, development, sales, marketing, and more, managed by a project leader, and given the needed resources,

When one is deprived of one's liberty, one is right in blaming not so much the man who puts the shackles on as the one who had the power to prevent him, but did not use it.

—Thucydides, *History of the Peloponnesian War*

can create and launch a product. A high-performing team achieves an output greater than the sum of its individual parts. This concept has been well documented.

In an article by Steven Tobak, "Making a Team Greater than the Sum of its Parts," he uses the analogy of graphite under pressure eventually becoming a diamond.[155]

However, a consistently replicable formula for such a team remains elusive. The team is a microcosm, a reflection of the organization as a whole, the macrocosm.

The structure of a team emulates that of the organization; it has rules, or acceptable and expected behavior, called norms. An example of a norm is the expectation that all members of the team will deliver their part of the overall task on time, or meetings are to be no longer than an hour, beginning and ending promptly. No team can be successful achieving its goals without adequate resources from the macro or larger organization. Such resources include clearly-defined goals, sufficient time, money, training, strong leadership and executive champions that maintain the project as part of the company's overall strategic plan. Most teams fail due to limits being placed on any one of these resources leaving team members emotionally deflated and the client dissatisfied. After a project, teams often neglect to debrief and learn from the experience—what went right or did not work. Such learning experiences are wasted if not discussed and documented.[156]

In his bestselling book, *The Fifth Discipline*, Peter Senge describes a learning organization as "a place where people continually expand their capacity to create the results they truly desire—where new and expansive patterns of thinking are nurtured; where people are continually learning."[157] You can amass the highest performers, but without adequate resources—staff, time and money— the team will flounder.

I think every leader has an obligation—the absolute obligation—to treat everyone fairly. But they also have the obligation to treat everyone differently. Because people aren't all the same, and the last thing you ever want to do, in my opinion, is let the best in your organization be treated like the worst in your organization. It does nothing for your future.

—Jack Welch

Groups versus Teams: Four Stages of Group Development

Since we spend most of our time working and living in and among groups of people, I believe having insight into group behavior is an important source of learning how to better communicate and manage conflict.

Groups can be defined as two or more people working together with a common goal: formal, such as work groups, and informal, such as church groups.

In Bruce Tuckman's seminal work published in 1965, *Developmental Sequence in Small Groups*,[158] he describes the four stages of group development: forming, storming. norming and performing. A fifth stage, adjourning, was later added in 1977. The time frames between each stage can occur over varying periods. The impetus for Tuckman's research was to observe groups in long-term settings, and the groups identified in Tuckman's research were typically formed for psychological and therapeutic analysis, led by a counselor. The participants in these groups were in a leader-member or counselor-patient relationship.

The *forming* stage occurs when members of the group first gather, get to know each other and find their place among the other members. In the next stage, *storming*, conflicts arise when group members object to control by other members and lack formal leadership. The *norming* stage is characterized by members sharing a sense of belonging and a desire to build a structure with norms and goal identification. Some examples of norms: Respond to messages within 24 hours; be present at all team meetings; copy all team members on communications. *Performing* is the third stage typified by the completion of the group's goal. When the group disbands, it has reached its fifth and final stage, adjourning.[159] When teaching project management,

I emphasized the importance of a post-completion briefing to document what worked and did not work in the execution of a task. Such information is valuable in the database of future projects.

I have engaged extensively with work teams as a consultant and as a professor overseeing academic groupwork. I have consulted with work teams for as long as ten years or as brief as eight weeks. Most job-related "teams" today are high performing and brought together because of diverse and expert skills—under tremendous pressure to meet extremely short deadlines. Typically, a team of experts has resources, leadership and norms drawn from the culture of the organization. Such teams may work together only once or over a long term.

Have you ever ridden on mass transit and watched hundreds of people rush off the train then scurry to the base of the long escalators only to come to a halt, waiting in lines heading up the escalator? I've been in such a crowd and equated my experience analogous to groups trying to get things done, yet thwarted by the slowest, least educated or ill-prepared member. (See the following section on social loafing.) My analogy is not a put-down but an honest statement. In the emergency department the flow can be thwarted by a clerk forgetting to ensure an order is completed or forgetting to document an appointment and the patient arrives to learn about this oversight. Either the schedule is adjusted or the patient reschedules—both options obstruct patient flow.

I used the Group Effectiveness Model presented in Roger Swartz book, *The Skilled Facilitator*, when teaching about team building.[160] The model is rich with content derived from the seminal research of the original contributors to the study of groups and work teams. Jay Lorch and Arthur Walker, in their 1968 influential article, "Organizational Choice: Product versus Function," posed the question of whether work teams perform best when segregated by product or function.[161] Today, we have a combination of both. In the 1970s, I was an early example of teams being built by both function and product. My function was as a nurse, however, I represented the product of delivering emergency care to patients. Sundstrom, De Meuse and Futrell also influenced the foundation of research on work teams. Their publication, "Work Teams: Application and Effectiveness," concluded that group effectiveness is more than meeting a goal, but addressed how the member felt once the team disbanded.[162] The terms "process and personal" were added to the assessment of team member satisfaction upon dispersing. Did the member want to work with this group of individuals again, and how did the member feel about him/herself at the conclusion of the project? In order for a group/team to be effective, it must have a working mission and total support, in the form of resources, from the organization. It is not uncommon for an organization to bring together a cross-functional team with a scope, goal and budget, only to abandon the team by limiting human and monetary resources. When the C-suite advises you that team members' participation will be limited, the budget more restrictive and you'll have to work without a project manager, you know the organization's strategic plan is no longer supporting your project.

Jack Welch, past CEO of General Electric (GE) and author of *Winning*, identifies eight winning strategies of a leader. Jack Welch led by being transparent, believing you must be the example of how you want staff to behave. He believed in building a peak-performing team by being ever vigilant in providing the needed resources, listening and garnering member opinions, communicating his vision into every action he took.[163]

Jack Welch believed in building a high-performing team by bringing the middle-performers up to excel as well as the top 20 percent

> *Before you are a leader success is all about growing yourself.*
> *When you are a leader success is all about growing others.*
>
> —Jack Welch

performers. Welch insured all the coaching, training and resources were provided for the other 70 percent of his employees, and letting go of the 10 percent of the low-performers. He believed that, "Protecting underperformers always backfires."

Social Loafing

The intrusion of weeds devouring resources from the intended roses and stressing its roots, reminds me of individuals who rob team members of valuable resources, especially time. In organizational theory the term for this behavior is social loafing. We have all experienced the inadequate performance of social loafers and how their behavior stresses team members and their output. For years I taught courses in group dynamics and team building, and did a great deal of consulting related to these subjects. My classroom became a working laboratory for practicing group effectiveness. Groups of students were given projects to simulate a team in the workplace. At least half of the groups came to me complaining that one or two members were not performing their share of the work—mind you these are graduate and doctoral students. My classroom was no different than the workgroups I encountered while consulting. The weak members of a team rob the rest of the team, depleting the energy from members who will not allow the team to do poorly. Organizations will lose good performers if the social loafers are not "weeded out."

CONFLICT: LADDER OF INFERENCE

Can you recall a time when you misinterpreted the actions of someone that led you to behave in a disrespectful way— only later to regret such an attitude? Chris Argyris, whom I've noted earlier, provides us with the "Ladder of Inference," a metaphor for how we create conclusions that may lead to conflict based upon a single, simple observed act.[164] How many times has an action of a coworker, partner, friend or simple acquaintance led you to deduce the motivation of their actions, and, in turn influenced you to take a series of actions based upon the original deduction? Let me explain using a personal example.

Protecting underperformers always backfires.

—Jack Welch

I was teaching a group of graduate students when throughout the class I observed a student looking at his watch and sending texts when I was lecturing. Not only was it distracting, it felt disrespectful. The student started to shuffle his papers before class ended, then hurried out as soon as I dismissed class. I was annoyed at his lack of participation and obvious distraction. This behavior was repeated in the next class. Since he never approached me to explain his actions, I assumed he was not interested in the course. The student missed the next class without letting me know his reason. I was now going to reduce his grade according to the guidelines of the syllabus.

Let's see how I climbed the Ladder of Inference according to Chris Argyris (see page 262). First, I experienced "observable data." Looking at his watch, shuffling papers, texting, leaving class immediately. The second rung of the Ladder, "selected data," was achieved by shedding all the data except the conclusion that the student's behavior was

7 take action

6 update beliefs

5 draw conclusions

4 make assumptions

3 add meanings

2 selected data

1 observable data

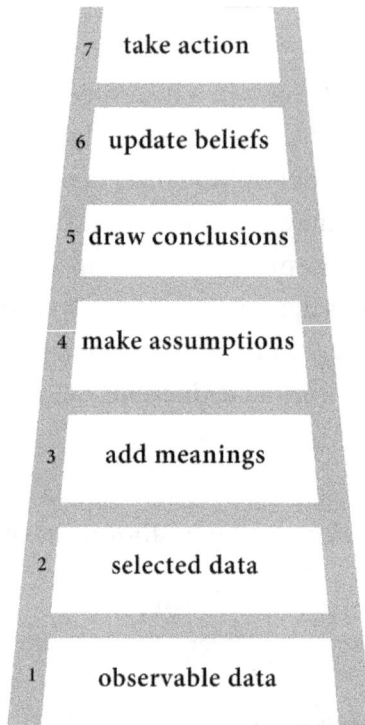

directly targeted toward me. Mental models, or predetermined ideas about people based upon previous personal experiences or biases, led me to the "assumptions" that the student's behavior was that of disrespect for me and a lack of interest in the course. In doing so, I "added meaning" to the student's behavior. I now quickly climb the Ladder to draw "conclusions" by reinforcing my convictions, or "adopting my beliefs" that this student is rude, a slacker and just putting in his time in class. I now step to the top of the ladder and "take action" to reduce the student's grade (according to the syllabus—a contract between the student and professor), for lack of participation and missing class. Now that I have quickly risen to the top of the ladder without face-to-face communication, let's take a look at a different strategy that reverses the actions taken and come down the Ladder toward a better outcome.

Steps up the Ladder of Inference and Conflict

First, *observable data*—Relatively directly observable data, such as: looked at watch, squirming in chair and looking at feet.

Second, *selected data*—The only person who left in a hurry (based on my mental models); no eye contact with me when he leaves; doesn't mix with the other students; poor participation.

Third, *add meanings*—Bored, uninterested, doesn't like the class, doesn't like me.

Fourth, *make assumptions*—He had to take this class and really could care less about content; or he thinks the course content is too lightweight compared to his other courses.

Fifth, *draw conclusions* that leads to beliefs—He's probably an under-achiever and will under-perform in this class; he will want an incomplete.

Sixth, *update beliefs* that lead to actions—still looking at his phone a lot; no participation during class; this is the second time he's left class early, so stop giving him opportunities.

Seventh, *take action*—He will receive no participation points, even though he did attend class—resulting in a half-grade drop.[165]

Climbing Back Down the Ladder: Make it a Win/Win

The key ingredient to reversing the rapid climb up the Ladder is through "self-awareness."[166] At each rung of the Ladder, particularly at the observable data rung, I failed to ask why this student was behaving as he did. I chose only to focus on his ill-mannered behavior, thus leading me quickly up the Ladder based upon my experiences, assuming his behavior was all about me, the professor, versus him. Rather than step back and question my "assumptions," then "conclusions" and ultimate "action," I went straight up the Ladder without ever "communicating" with this student.

In this case, I made a lot of assumptions based on little information and never questioned the assumptions I made without firsthand data. Start with observations not assumptions.

Now, let's look at how I came back down the Ladder. First, I became aware of the fact that I never really communicated with the student. More importantly, I drew conclusions without putting myself in his place—I observed the entire situation, step-by-step up the Ladder. I reached a conclusion about the student's behavior based upon my assumptions and without ever getting to know him or trying to understand what was prompting his behavior.

When we finally spoke, I heard him describe the prior three weeks waiting for his third child. His wife was pregnant and considered a high-risk pregnancy. He had two children under three at home and was worried about getting home to be there to relieve his wife. He was shaken by all the responsibility placed on him at the same time he undertook his graduate degree. He explained the texting and rapid escape from class was a result of concern for maintaining his commitment as an expectant father. His wife would deliver soon and he assured me coursework would be on time and better attention would be paid in class. As a result of our discussion, and an opportunity for both of us to express our positions, the end result was a win/win.

Ask yourself why you created such assumptions and ignored all feedback other than what you chose. Our experiences lead us to our beliefs.

How do we climb back down the Ladder? We need self-awareness— ask ourselves what else could be going on in the subject's life versus what we concluded? What are our belief systems and mental models contributing to this reaction? Openly communicate to avert conflict.

Pondy's Model of Conflict

I introduce Louise Pondy's Model of Conflict in this book for two reasons: The Model recognizes that conflict is ever-present and simply waiting to emerge, and that conflict must be managed at an early stage to avoid harmful consequences. The Model consists of five stages: latent, perceived, felt, manifest and aftermath.[167]

Latent conflict lies dormant as a tension awaiting to materialize, most likely, between teams or departments in an organization. The *perception stage* occurs when there is an awareness that another department or group views resources or other advantages have been given to a competing group in a different part of the organization. At the *felt stage*, no action is taken but emotional undercurrent exists. One organizational design method is the creation of cross-functional teams, deflecting rivalry among multiple departments with competing goals within an organization. Next, the *manifest stage* occurs when evidence of one group thwarting another group's goals occurs and one team takes an action against another to impede their goals. If the growing conflict is not managed at the early stages an employee leaves or is fired.

Reflect in Your Garden

As you walk among nature, take an assessment of any conflicts you may have created by misinterpreting the actions of a coworker, family member, partner or acquaintance. How did miscommunication/lack of communication affect the outcome of the conflict?

How are you selecting the data observed or heard when working/ living with others that influences how you respond to a coworker, family member, partner or acquaintance?

The next time you're in a meeting with coworkers take an internal assessment of biases you may bring to the meeting. Are you able to leave these mental models in abeyance the next time you meet?

How has social media impacted your ability to communicate effectively and influenced the mental models you have added to your database? With regard to conflict, how has social media improved or hindered your ability to communicate in face-to-face interactions?

Reflect upon a recent situation in which a conflict between you and a coworker/family member erupted due to self-selected data and you climbing the ladder of inference. How are you now able to manage the conflict before you reach the final rung on the ladder?

How are walks among flowers, a bike ride, or any activity in nature that inspire calm and allow time for reflection, a means to avoid conflict in your life?

So much of what we call management consists of making it difficult for people to work.

—Peter Drucker

Using my healthcare background, let me illustrate Pondy's Model of Conflict. A common source of organizational disputes is an asymmetry of goals among workers and their departments. Hospitals are no different and I can speak firsthand regarding the stages of conflict that frequently arise during the goal of moving patients efficiently from the emergency department to the critical care units. The critical care areas, intensive and coronary care, also have their goals of maintaining quality care of their inpatients. It appears all should go well between these departments, yet how each department achieves its goals doesn't necessarily work in coordination with each other. Consider also that while the overarching goal of the hospital is patient care, the central focus is the budget, which sometimes gets in the way of appropriate decision-making (recall the driving and restraining forces). In summary, we have three disparate goals that Pondy describes as *stage one, latent conflict.*

It's not uncommon for all beds in the emergency department to be occupied, with a full waiting room of patients, and ambulances coming in with emergent patients. This gridlock is often only relieved by moving patients to critical care units; the units, in turn, must move patients to less critical beds or discharge home. This ongoing shifting of patients is the primer to create the *second stage, perceived conflict.* When intensive care tells the emergency department staff they have no beds, and the hospital supervisor wants to wait until the next shift to call in more nurses to staff empty beds, a perception among emergency department staff is that there is a lack of support from critical care and the hospital supervisor to decompress the emergency department. We've now moved to the *third, felt stage,* according to Pondy. In order to keep patients moving in the emergency department, emergency department management "accommodate" by calling in more staff, putting patients in the hall; but resentment builds and a sense of abandonment spreads quickly among the emergency department nurses.

When an intensive care nurse tells the emergency department nurse to further accommodate the critical care nurses by "waiting an additional 30 minutes before transferring a patient upstairs to the ICU while reports are given [between outgoing and oncoming nurses]," the conflict escalates to the *fourth, manifest stage.* This is the tipping point for an already frustrated emergency nurse who now decides she's going to take a patient to the intensive care despite their request. When she arrives in the ICU, no one is there to transfer the patient, and an angry ICU nurse files a formal complaint against the emergency department nurse.

Because of a breakdown in communication between the managing nurses of both departments, and the failure of the hospital's nursing supervisor to appropriately intervene with support for both departments, disagreements escalate to a serious, perhaps dangerous, *conflict aftermath stage.* The eventual result, in this case, of such mismanagement could result in specialized nurses quitting or being fired, and/or, a worse-case scenario: a patient incident and lawsuit.

Conflict must be managed! Collaboration versus competition, compromise versus accommodation.[168] To remedy the above dispute between two critical care areas and the hospital's budgetary priorities, cross-functionally prepared nurses were developed. Nurses who worked both in the emergency department and ICU quelled the ever-present tension, getting a firsthand appreciation for the challenges faced by the opposition. Also, a team of nurses simply observed the opposite department, and, finally, a group of representatives from all departments met regularly to discuss and resolve issues as they arose, dissipating disagreements before they escalated.

ACTION SCIENCE

Action Science is another methodology introduced by Chris Argyris to improve communication among team members. The process is one that is learned and takes place over time. However, like the Ladder of Inference, at its core is self-awareness, particularly among a group of individuals gathered together to complete a project. This core of individuals can be anything from a sports team, religious group, ensemble cast, or work cohort, all brought together to produce a group outcome.[169]

Mental Models 1 and 2

Chris Argyris describes *two mental models, 1 and 2.* Mental Model 1 is destructive, exclusive, and a win/lose. In this paradigm, individuals impede communication (and by extension, relationships) and sabotage outcomes. Mental Model 1 includes, per Argyris, "undiscussing the undiscussable," individuals' reticence to question, mixed messages, unilateral tasks, and competition toward isolation. Once again, Chris Argyris refers to this as single-loop behavior, as opposed to questioning, self-awareness, recognizing one's biases or mental models.

A description of Mental Model 2: feeling safe to ask questions, bilateral decision-making with all members contributing to the team's common goal, and a secure sense that communication is among all team members for purposes of producing the best outcome of the group. I would suggest that in the Mental Model 2 framework, the outcome produced is greater than the sum-total of the individual members. This team model is considered high-performing in organizational behavior group dynamics. Chris Argyris describes this Mental Model 2 as utilizing his double-loop thinking, encouraging one to question the norm and shift the paradigm to a new way of examining/executing.[170]

Reflect in Your Garden

Have you created a business culture around group effectiveness (vs. social loafing); is teamwork evident as opposed to individuals getting ahead?

How have you set your employees up for success? Do you offer employee development via ongoing training and education stipends?

How are you a resource for the individuals who report to you? Or do you micromanage your staff?

How often do you seek input from your employees regarding their work and ideas to make your company better?

Do you provide ongoing evaluations with measurable goals that are aligned with the vision of the company?

Coda on Coronavirus

The white-crowned sparrow sang at a pitch not heard since the 1970s in San Francisco. The absence of noise during the coronavirus (Covid-19) allowed the birds to communicate with their loved ones 60 miles away versus 15 feet during pre-pandemic times.[171]

Less ships during Covid-19 meant less din and its frequencies disrupting communication among marine life. A biological oceanographer at the Monterey Bay Area Research Institute (MBARI), John Ryan, documented that, *The sound of global trade is in the ocean and that sound is noise. Ocean noise levels responded quickly to economic impacts of the pandemic.* Ryan also stated, *Noise is an ephemeral pollutant.* Without the noise the quality of marine life improves.[172]

Researchers called the quiet "anthropause." Seismologists were able to measure a reduction in seismic movement as deep as 1,300 feet, the direct result of reduced traffic and chaotic movement of human activity. Scientists documented a 50 percent reduction in ground noise—equivalent to a loud conversation reduced to a whisper. The whispers brought mountain lions into neighborhoods to birth their babies and the coyotes, raccoons, bobcats and even deer are the new pedestrians. Chris Wilmes, a professor at the University of California at Santa Cruz and part of the Santa Cruz Puma Project, documented that mountain lions avoided urban areas pre-Covid-19 and have retreated post-pandemic.[173]

Other headlines read: "A group of Orca whales never seen behaving in such an aggressive manner ramming boats causing bodily harm to the mariners off the coasts of Spain and Portugal.[174] Sharks swarming close to the Central California beaches and an unprecedented death of a surfer from a great white shark attack this summer near the beach break in Santa Cruz County.[175] [176]

August 2020, fires have burned over 3.3 million acres of land in California, a size comparable to that of the state of Connecticut. More fires spread along Oregon and Washington's coast, with more than 30 deaths attributed to these vast infernos.[177]

As fast as the wildfires are spreading, so are efforts to "defund" police and a growing hatred of the "men in blue"—the same first responders lauded after September 11, 2001.

COMPLEXITY THEORY? THE PSYCHOSOCIAL FALLOUT OF COVID-19

My friend in Goa, India tells me there is a surge in crime in her area. In San Francisco, New York and Chicago the murder rate increased by 40 percent in 2020 with crime intensifying over half the United States, while ammunition sales have skyrocketed.[178 179 180]

Racial tensions erupted, the underpinnings of riots across the country, spawning uprisings across the world—the extent of which has never been seen. Anti-fascism (Antifa) rebels took over a six-block area in Seattle, Washington in June 2020, referred to as the Capitol Hill Occupied Precinct (CHOP) Autonomous Zone, and more outbreaks of these rebellions multiply throughout the country.[181 182]

COVID-19 led to a startling rise in the rate of suicide while sober addicts experienced drug and alcohol recidivism as a result of being sheltered in place. In San Francisco, 713 deaths were attributed to accidental overdoses, double the rate of 2019 and over two times more than the 257 deaths due to COVID-19.[183] According to the National Institutes of Health COVID-19 has added stress, anxiety, depression and feelings of isolation that will continue well beyond the end of the pandemic.[184] Respondents to a Centers for Disease Control (CDC) survey in June 2020 reported an increase in drug abuse, adverse mental health conditions and ideations of suicide.[185]

Clearly the cause and effect of extraordinary events are interconnected.

The rolling statistics were spread across TVs tallying the minute-by-minute COVID-19 cases and deaths; an ever-present reminder of the vulnerability of each observer. (Close to my home the last COVID-19 death was catalogued as a 90 plus year old in hospice).

At the start of the pandemic those close to me were on "high alert," as everyone looked right to left and left to right, as if I and others were leaving droplets of an unwelcomed virus. Hidden behind masks we lined up outside stores until an acceptable number were allowed to enter. Showers of disinfectants sprayed across carts as lines are cordoned in six-foot spaces. Restaurants were graveyards of what was as tables and chairs were stacked along the walls until those in power gave the okay to reopen. People with shredded nerves were clawing for normalcy.

Ten percent of the country's restaurants closed permanently as a result of COVID-19.[186] In San Francisco, 48 percent of small businesses closed and 34 percent across America, since January 2020.[187]

For some, a crisis meant an opportunity. Telemedicine—healthcare delivery through virtual means—rose 154 percent in March 2020 from the same time in 2019.[188] Streaming services rose, as did sales of supplies for home repair. "App" drivers such as Uber, Lyft and Door Dash had a symbiotic relationship with restaurants who both financially benefited from home delivery. Restaurants continue to redefine how they deliver food—some are abandoning their brick and mortar locations for kitchens and delivery-only functions. Online retailers and grocery businesses rose exponentially. No online retailer, or business for that matter, expanded more than Amazon adding hundreds of thousands of new employees to its ranks and hiring every available cargo plane to meet the exponential demand during COVID-19.[189]

When I embarked upon writing this book four years ago, after a decade-long inspiration to document my observations of the interrelationships between nature and business, I concluded a far-reaching connection between all living systems, extending beyond the universes we can observe. When the Covid-19 pandemic raged upon the world, I could find no better example of this vast connection between the smallest cell to the edges of the cosmic infinity.

In addition to the loss of lives, perhaps the most deleterious impact of the pandemic, when we eventually open our doors and remove our masks, will be the economic fallout and its impact on generations to come.

The government has printed money to lessen the financial losses of business owners and employees, and, without a doubt, the trillions of dollars of new debt will burden our children and children's children.

As of this writing, seven trillion dollars were allocated to Covid-19 relief—U.S. debt is $30 trillion dollars.

The extensive cause and effect and unintended consequences of Covid-19 include economic and demographic changes. Individuals and companies have changed their business designs to encourage and/or require staff to work from home. Research, *Why Working from Home Will Stick*, estimates 20 percent of workers, versus 5 percent pre-Covid-19, will continue to work from home.[190] Such policy changes have led to an exodus from expensive, densely populated areas such as the San Francisco Bay Area to oceanside communities, some even leaving the state entirely.

Schools and universities abruptly closed—the impact on academic progress over the last several years will play out for years to come, and has forced institutions of learning, as well as students, to rethink the methodology of delivering education.

The 20 million plus who filed unemployment are trickling back to work. Employers are begging for workers while employees have changed occupations to ensure an "essential" work status or remain at home collecting far more on unemployment. A new idiom has emerged, "the great resignation," among workers who are dissatisfied with the quality and pay of their current jobs. An analysis of 9,000 employees and 4,000 world-wide companies found many to be from the healthcare and tech industries.[191] Among those not returning to work are 55 to 64 year old workers who have decided to retire earlier than planned. Covid-19 has stimulated a rethinking of priorities, the fragility of life—establishing new goals. Yet, another example of cause and effect.

Again, what better example of systems theory than the cause and effects from Covid-19. A single cause ripples into an infinite series of effects—suddenly aborting day-to-day dependence on systems we took for granted such as driving to work, attending school, the purchasing of needed goods—a loss of freedoms. Unquestioningly, we were shuddered into a seemingly secure place and all available resources poured into ensuring a viable, ever-ready healthcare system to treat all comers. However, despite our "best efforts" the pandemic cost the lives of over 600,000 people in the United States.

Clearly the cause and effect of extraordinary events, to further attest to my belief, and thesis of this book, that all living things are interconnected. Nature and that which governs nature are our ultimate teachers.

Interconnected

The house was intact
until the earth beneath it shuddered
was there no room to assimilate—
after all, who was here first

the house topples
the earth below remains
this space yours
for billions of years

new life erupts
the perfumed rose draws us near
entangled mint tendrils run deep
each plant touches the other—sovereign or symbiotic

the ocean sings a chorus
to the tilts of the trees
as the insects pause to listen—

all life is interconnected

Summary

I have come to the end of a writing journey that began four years ago, however, the inspiration to create this book began nearly 15 years ago as a I poured my grief into creating an expansive garden after the passing of my father. Upon reflection, I have no doubt my father influenced my thoughts as I have compiled *Nature to Business: Wisdom from My Garden*. Even as I complete the final pages of this book, my senses pique and my mind fills with new inspirations each time I step into my garden—revelations I'll continue to share on my website's blog: Kathleennakfoor.com

As I scattered the seeds, dug the bulbs into place and planted the bare root roses across the fresh laid soil, the thoughts emerged without provocation and led me to see the parallels between the rules of nature and how people behave in organizations. Mother Nature is our teacher as the cycles in a business progress as the cycles in nature unfold. Observing these similarities led me to conclude that all living things are interrelated.

Whether the "seed" of a start-up or the undeveloped seed of a rose, neither is put into place until a design is created and the risks are mitigated. Growth is only feasible with a culture that feeds its core.

We need a strategic plan in our personal and business life—a dynamic roadmap to our overarching mission and vision. Utilize the nine steps in PlanKit®, its business tools and prompts for self-reflection, to create a blueprint that will *move you and your business from where you are to where you want to be.* Keep in mind that the strategic plan you create using PlanKit® is dynamic. Revisit your plan, at least annually, and use the nine steps including the Force Field Analysis, cause and effect diagram, reinforcing and balancing loops and Porter's Model of Five Forces, to keep your plan on track.

Effective leaders are authentic, who take time for reflection and highly regard their human resources—the conduit to quality customer service. A successful leader spends more time out of the office and face-to-face with her employees and customers ascertaining their needs than sitting behind a desk. To understand and successfully lead your staff is to provide needed resources, mitigate conflict before it escalates and be mindful of the power of the informal organization. We need more servant leaders and those who spend time in quiet thought among nature.

We must learn to communicate better and design our organizations without boundaries for honest and constructive expression of ideas. I believe that poor communication is the root cause of most complex systems' problems.

The relevance of systems theory is the gateway to understanding a plausible, scientific rationale for how a single cell is connected to the expanding universes—how our daily routines intersect an infinite number of complex systems. Without an understanding of the interrelationships among the multiple sub-systems we are unable to permanently resolve a problem at its root cause.

Reflecting on my thesis, the interrelatedness of all living things became clearer the more I embarked upon the subject. The misfortunes left as a result of COVID-19 descended upon us like blunt trauma leaving a world acutely aware of the tentativeness of life, and how connected we are across the globe.

Does the exceptional virulence of the coronavirus arouse a new appreciation for Edward Lorenz' chaos theory—such an exceptional example of how small changes thousands of miles away create a storm across the world?

I point to complexity and chaos theories for answers as to why on January 6, 2021 large numbers of marchers breached the United States Capitol and the civil unrest that erupted across major cities in the United States in 2020.

Throughout *Nature to Business: Wisdom from My Garden*, you have been exposed to a plethora of theory and business tools that are immediately transferable to your business. I encourage you to incorporate Chris Argyris' ideas on how to better communicate and manage conflict among staff. I urge you to reflect on how effective your organization's design is in promoting optimal communication and productivity, and how well you support your staff's growth and development through the efficacious provision of adequate resources.

I have provided the organizational theory, augmented with years of my experiences cultivating businesses and cultivating a garden. My hope is that you are inspired to see the world in a new way—to adapt and change—to realize a successful business and personal life are only possible by developing and nurturing relationships.

The earth and nature have existed for billions of years and have shown us its ability to adapt and heal far beyond the capabilities of man. It is my hope that you will spend time in nature contemplating the reflective prompts throughout the book. Mother Nature has much to teach us that we must learn. Without freedom we cannot learn, without learning we cannot survive.

My book is intended to be a lifelong reference; to probe, to teach, to inspire thought and to question. Don't ignore the pushes and pulls while you listen to nature for the answers.

Glossary

Action research—Studies carried out in the course of an activity or occupation to improve the methods and approach of those involved in a change process; collecting data during a process, analyzed then making change based upon the analysis of data collected.

Analysis—A detailed examination of anything complex in order to understand its nature or to determine its essential features; a thorough study.

Argyris, Chris—Chris Argyris (July 16, 1923 – November 16, 2013) was an American business theorist and professor emeritus at Harvard Business School. Argyris, like Richard Beckhard, Edgar Schein and Warren Bennis, is known as a co-founder of organization development, and known for seminal work on learning organizations.

Artifact—Something characteristic of or resulting from a particular human institution, period, trend, or individual.

App-based driver—Typically an independent contractor who performs various tasks involving driving and directed by individuals ordering such service via a software application provided by companies such as Uber, Lyft, Door Dash.

Balancing loop—A circle of cause and effect that counter a change with a push in the opposite direction. The goal of a balancing loop is to move from an existing state to a desired state through some action. One of the two interrelated parts of a learning system.

Bases of Power—Legitimate, coercive, expert, referent, information and charismatic.

Business cycle—A cycle of economic activity usually consisting of recession, recovery, growth, and decline; start-up, growth, establishment, maturity and decline.

Change theory—One model of change is Kurt Lewin's 3-step model of unfreezing, change, freezing; three types are static, dynamic and dynamical. See also John Kotter's change management.

Chaos—The property that characterizes a dynamical system in which most orbits exhibit sensitive dependence

Chaos theory—The branch of mathematics that deals with complex systems whose behavior is highly sensitive to slight changes in conditions, so that small alterations can give rise to strikingly great consequences.

Closed system—A concept of thermodynamics in which only energy can enter or leave the system; the system is self-sustaining without resources from its environment.

Communication—A process by which information is exchanged between individuals through a common system of symbols, signs, or behavior.

Complex adaptive theory—part of complexity theory; systems with their own set of unique rules: no locus of control; can be embedded in larger systems; i.e. cells; small changes create significant results; self-organize; interrelationship among parts are more important than individual parts; total is greater than individual parts; thrive on instability.

Complexity theory—see complex adaptive theory and chaos theory.

Culture—The customary beliefs, social forms, and material traits of a racial, religious, or social group; the set of shared attitudes, values, goals, and practices that characterize an institution or organization.

Ecosystem—A complex community of organisms and its environment functioning as an ecological unit; something (such as a network of businesses) considered to resemble an ecological ecosystem especially because of its complex interdependent parts.

Entropy—Thermodynamics: a measure of the unavailable energy in a closed thermodynamic system that is also usually considered to be a measure of the system's disorder, that is a property of the system's state, and that varies directly with any reversible change in heat in the system and inversely with the temperature of the system; the degree of disorder in a system. The degradation of the matter and energy in the universe to an ultimate state of inert uniformity. A process of degradation or running down of a trend to disorder.

Floribunda—Any of various usually small, compact roses with large flowers in open clusters that derive from crosses of polyantha and tea roses.

Flow—Motivational researchers describe as a state of being when time passes without notice because you're so engrossed in an activity that nothing seems to matter.

Force Field Analysis Model—Theory that forces exist between 2 bodies not in contact that fills the space. Driving forces that direct behavior away from the status quo in the direction we want to pursue versus restraining forces that keep us from moving in the direction of a goal; A systematic approach to describing behavior in patterns and the interactions are seen as forces (see also field theory).

Fungus—Any of a kingdom (Fungi) of saprophytic and parasitic spore-producing eukaryotic typically filamentous organisms formerly classified as plans that lack chlorophyll and include molds, rusts, mildews, smuts, mushrooms and yeasts.

   a. **Black spot**—Any of several bacterial or fungal diseases of plants characterized by black spots or blotches especially on the leaves.

   b. **Rust**—Any of numerous destructive diseases of plants produced by fungi and characterized by usually reddish-brown pustular lesions.

Gap Analysis—The difference between some current state and a desired state.

Gig economy—A labor market characterized by short-term contract or freelance work.

Groupthink—Symptoms of communication failure that leads to poor decision making under pressure; phenomenon in which the norm for consensus overrides the realistic appraisal of alternative courses of action.

Hybrid tea rose—Any of numerous moderately hardy cultivated hybrid roses grown especially for their strongly recurrent bloom of large usually scentless flowers.

Informal group—Not formally structured; not part of the organizational chart; emerge because of a need for social contact; can become a powerful network.

Insecticide, natural—An agent that destroys insects using agents not harmful to the environment, such as Dawn Soap.

Kurt Lewin—psychologist instrumental in the creation of the field of organizational development and behavior as a practical field of social science including theories of change and team building; force field analysis (FFA) and action research.

Ladder of Inference—A step-wise process, described by Chris Argyris, illustrating how conflict can build from a mere dismissive look to destructive behavior; steps are: observable data, selected data, add meaning, making assumptions, drawing conclusions, update beliefs, take action. Without skilled intervention and communication, the conflict may lead to one of the parties leaving the scene.

Leadership—The emergence, election or assignment of position of power; capacity to lead; the ability to influence a group toward the achievement of goal.

Learning organization—According to Peter Senge, who coined the term, "places where people expand their capacity to create and expand their pattern of thinking ; where people are continually learning to see the whole together."[192]

Open system—Open Systems are thought of as having both maintenance subsystems and adaptive mechanisms. The maintenance is to sustain the relationship between subsystems and hold the system together while adaptive mechanisms promote change so as to keep the system in dynamic equilibrium with the organization. Successful systems are able to deal with the paradox of stability and instability.

Opportunity Cost—The added cost of using resources (as for production or speculative investment) that is the difference between the actual value resulting from such use and that of an alternative (such as another use of the same resources or an investment of equal risk but greater return).

Organization—The act or process of organizing or of being organized; the condition or manner of being organized; an administrative and functional structure.

Organizational behavior—A field of study that investigates the impact that individuals, groups and structure have on the behavior within organizations, for the purpose of applying such knowledge toward improving an organization's effectiveness.

Organizational culture—Observable through artifacts, policies, communication, logo, organizational chart; a common perception held by employees; a system of shared meaning.

Organizational design/structure—The flow of communication among staff; determines reporting and decision-making authority.

Organizational development—A systemwide application and transfer of behavioral science knowledge to the planned development, improvement and reinforcement of the strategies, structures and processes that lead to organizational effectiveness.[193]

Organizational Learning—Organizational Learning is a knowledge area within organizational development theory that studies the way an organization learns and adapts using various models and theories sccording to Argyris and Schön (1978).

Paradigm shift—An important change that happens when the usual way of thinking about or doing something is replaced by a new and different way.

Pesticide, natural—An organic agent used to destroy pests.

Pondy's Model of Organizational Conflict—Five stages: latent, perceived, felt, manifest, conflict aftermath.

Porter's Five Forces Model—Created by Michael Porter as a method for assessing the forces of bargaining power of buyers and suppliers, threat of emerging businesses and threat of substitution.

Pre-emergence—Used or occurring before emergence of seedlings above the ground.

Reinforcing loop—A reinforcing loop represents an action within a system that produces a result which influences more of the same action—ultimately, resulting in growth or decline. One of the two interrelated parts of a learning system.

Rust and black spot on a rose—Any of numerous destructive diseases of plants produced by fungi and characterized by usually reddish-brown pustular lesions and/or black spots on the leaves of the plant.

Sector—A sociological, economic, or political subdivision of society.

S-curve—Sigmoid curve is a mathematical model illustrating the exponential growth and decline of a variable in terms of another variable and often expressed as units of time. For example, an S-curve during the growth of company, focusing on a new product launch, for a new product would show a rapid, exponential increase in sales for a period of time, followed by a tapering or leveling off.

Strategic plan—PlanKit® is used in this book to create a strategic plan using a nine-step model including the use of Lewin's Change Model, an examination of one's SWOT Analysis, core values, detailed short and long-term goals, force-field analysis (FFA) and Porter's Model of Five Forces; a business or personal overarching direction; dynamic and should be frequently monitored.

Sucker (rose)—A shoot from the roots or lower part of the stem of a plant below the root ball; if left in place can take over the original plant.

SWOT Analysis—An inventory of your internal strengths and weaknesses and the external opportunities and threats.

System—A regularly interacting or interdependent group of items forming a unified whole; any entity that can undergo variations of some sort as time progresses.

Systems theory—Systems theory is attributed to the work of Ludwig Bertalanffy; the interrelationships of the parts of a complex system is a means of problem solving; consists of inputs, transition, outputs and feedback; cohesive group of independent, yet interrelated parts that can be natural or man-made.

Team—The output of a team is typically greater than the sum of its parts, particularly in cross-functional, high-performing groups.

Recommended Reading

Argyris, C. (1993). *Knowledge for Action: A Guide to Overcoming Barriers to Organizational Change.* San Francisco, CA: Jossey-Bass Publishers

Argyris, C. (2000). *Flawed Advice and the Management Trap: How Managers Can Know When They're Getting Good Advice and When They're Not.* Oxford, UK: Oxford University Press

Argyris, C. (1982). *Reasoning, Learning, and Action: Individual and Organizational.* San Francisco: Jossey-Bass

Argyris, C. (2010). *Organizational Traps: Leadership, Culture, Organizational Design.* Oxford, UK: Oxford University Press

Argyris, C. (1973). *Intervention Theory a Method: A Behavioral Science View.* Reading, MA: Addison-Wesley Publishing Company

Argyris, C., & Schon, D. (1996). *Organizational Learning II.* Reading: Addison Wesley.

Austin, D. (1988). *The Heritage of the Rose.* England: Antique Collectors' Club

Beckard, R., Harris, R.T., *Organizational Transitions: Managing Complex Change,* 2nd ed. New York, NY: Additions Wesley OD Series

Bennis, W. (1999). *Managing People is like Herding Cats.* Provo, UT: Executive Excellence Publishing

Bennis, W. (2002). *Geeks & Geezers: How Era, Values, and Defining Moments Shape Leaders.* Boston, MA: Harvard Business School Press

Block, P. (1993). *Stewardship: Choosing Service Over Self-Interest.* San Francisco, CA: Barrett-Koehler

Brenzel, Kathleen N. (2007). *Sunset, Western Garden Book.* 8th ed. Menlo Park, CA: Sunset Publishing Corporation

Bridges, W. (1991). *Managing Transitions: Making the Most of Change,* 3rd ed. Philadelphia: DeCapo Press

Collins, J. (2001). *Good to Great.* New York, NY: Harper Collins Press

Covey, S. (1990). *Principle Centered Leadership.* New York, NY: Simon and Shuster

Csikszentmihalyi, M. (1997). *Finding Flow: The Psychology of Engagement with Everyday Life.* New York: Basic Books

Csikszentmihalyi, M. (2003). *Good Business: Leadership, Flow and the Making of Meaning.* New York ,NY: Penguin Group

Drucker, P. F. (2002). *Managing in the Next Society.* New York, NY: St. Martin's Press

Drucker, P.F. (1995). *Managing in a Time of Great Change.* New York, NY: Penguin Books, USA, Inc.

Drucker, P. (2010). *Frontiers of Management: Where Tomorrows Decisions are Shaped Today.* Boston, MA: Harvard Business Review Press

Drucker, P. (2001). *The Essential Drucker.* New York, NY: Harper Collins Press

Drucker, P. (1985). *Innovation and Entrepreneurship.* New York, NY: Harper Collins

Drucker, P. (1990). *Managing the Non-Profit Organization: Principles and Practices.* New York: Harper Collins Press

Drucker, P. (1973). *Management: Tasks, Responsibilities, Practices.* New York, NY: Harpers Collins Publishers, Inc.

French, W., Bell, C. H. Jr. (1978). *Organizational Development: Behavioral Science Interventions for Organizational Improvement.* 2nd ed. Englewood Cliffs, NJ: Prentice Hall, Inc.

Harvard Business Review on Change (1991). Boston, MA: Harvard Business Press

Hammer, Michael, Champy, James (1993). *Reengineering the Organization: A Manifesto for Business Revolution.* New York: Harper Business

Hesselbein, F., Godsmith, M., Beckard, R. Ed. (1997), *The Organization of the Future by The Drucker Foundation.* San Francisco, CA: Jossey-Bass

Moss Kanter, R. (2004). *Confidence: How Winning Streaks and Losing Streaks Begin and End.* New York, NY: Crown Business.

Kotter, J.P. (2012). *Leading Change.* Boston, MA: Harvard Business Review Press

Kotter, J.P. (2002). *The Heart of Change.* Boston, MA: Harvard Business Review Press

Kouzes, J. M., Posner, B. Z. (1995). *The Leadership Challenge: How to Keep Getting Extraordinary Things Done in Organizations.* San Francisco, CA: Jossey-Bass

Mathew, Brian, Swindells, Philip. (1994). *The Complete Book of Bulbs: Corms, Tubers and Rhizomes.* Pleasantville, NY: Readers Digest Association, Inc.

Peters, T. (1994). *The Pursuit of WOW.* New York, NY: Vintage Books

Peters, T. (1994). *The Tom Peters Seminar.* New York, NY: Vintage Books

Renesch, J. Ed. (1994). *Leadership in a New Era: Visionary Approaches to the Biggest Crisis of Our Time.* San Francisco, CA: New Leaders Press

Schein, E. H. (1969). *Process Consultation, Its Role in Organization Development, Vol.1.* Reading, MA: Addison-Wesley Press

Schein, E. H. (1987). *Process Consultation, Lessons for Managers and Consultants, Vol.II.* Reading, MA: Addison-Wesley Press

Senge, P., Schein, E., et al, Ed. (1998). *The New Workplace: Transforming the Character and Culture of our Organizations.* Waltham, MA: Pegasus Communications, Inc.

Sull, D. (2003). *Revival of the Fittest: Why Good Companies Go Bad and How Great Managers Remake Them.* Boston, MA: Harvard Business School Press

Sunset Western Garden Solver: Companion to the Western Garden Book (1998). Menlo Park, CA: Sunset Publishing Corporation

Turner, R.J. Jr., Wasson, Ernie. ed. (1997). *Botanica: The Illustrated A-Z of Over 10,000 Garden Plants and How to Cultivate Them.* Miltons Point, Austrailia: Mynah

Wills, G. (1994), *Certain Trumpets: The Nature of Leadership.* New York, NY: Simon and Schuster

https://www.yumpu.com/en/document/view/49773204/wonderful-roses-our-water-our-world. (n.d.).

Endnotes

1. Schein, E., Kurt Lewin's Change Theory in the Field and in the Classroom: Notes toward a model of managed learning. *Systems Practice* 9, 27–47 (1996). https://doi.org/10.1007/BF02173417

2. Lewin, K. (1951). *Field theory in social science: selected theoretical papers (Edited by Darwin Cartwright.).* New York, NY: Harpers

3. https://hbr.org/1979/03/how-competitive-forces-shape-strategy

4. Porter, Michael E. (2008). The Five Competitive Forces That Shape Strategy. *Harvard Business Review*, p79-93

5. https://www.forbes.com/sites/theyec/2018/01/11/business-life-cycle-spectrum-where-are-you/#4cf2dcafef5e

6. Von Bertalanffy, L. (1968). *General Systems Theory: Foundations, Development, Application.* New York: George Braziller, Inc.

7. Kendal, R. Ed., Romer, B.S. trans (1989) Monet, Claude: *My Garden by Himself.* Great Britain, UK: Macdonald & Co.

8. Lorenz, E. (1993). *The Essence of Chaos.* Seattle, WA: University of Washington Press

9. *ibid*

10. Theodore Payne Foundation, FactSheetagvmwd.org/portals/0/documents/TPFCaliforniaNativePlants FactSheet.pdf

11. http://ferncreekdesign.org/backyardecosystem.html

12. *ibid*

13. https://wildlife.ca.gov/conservation/plants

14. https://planthardiness.ars.usda.gov/PHZMWeb/.

15. hbr.org the half-truths of first mover advantage, April 2001

16. https://farmhouseblooms.com/how-to-grow-roses-from-seed/

17. https://planthardiness.ars.usda.gov/PHZMWeb/

18. https://www.CMS.gov

19 https://www.cms.gov/Research-Statistics-Data-and-Systems/
Statistics-Trends-and-Reports/NationalHealthExpendData/NHE-
Fact-Sheet

20 https://www.fastcompany.com/40582757/why-paneras-experiment-
with-pay-what-you-want-dining-failed

21 Peters, Tom, Waterman, Robert H. Jr., (1982). *In Search of
Excellence.* Broadway: Harper-Collins

22 https://www.organiclesson.com/beneficial-insects-garden-pest-
control/

23 Plants Can Hear Themselves Being Eaten, and Can Communicate
the Threat to Their Neighbors, Dr. Mercola, https://articles.mercola.
com/sites/articles/archive/2014/10/11/plant-communication.aspx

24 https://www.thespruce.com/companion-planting-for-roses-1403041

25 https://www.theguardian.com/science/2018/may/02/plants-talk-to-
each-other-through-their-roots

26 Gorzelak, M, et al, *Inter-plant communication through mycorrhizal
mediates complex adaptive behavior in plant commu*nities. https://
www.ncbi.nlm.nih.gov/pmc/articles/PMC4497361

27 https://wildlife.ca.gov/conservation/plants

28 Riotte, L. (1998/1983). *Roses Love Garlic: Companion Planting and
Other Secrets of Flowers.* North Adams, MA: Storey Press

29 https://pdfslide.net/education/companion-planting-for-roses-the-new-
york-botanical-garden.html

30 Riotte, L, (1998). *Carrots Love Tomatoes.* North Adams, MA: Storey
Press

31 Drucker, P, Senge, P. *A Conversation with Peter Drucker and Peter
Senge: What it will take to Lead Tomorrow*

32 https://www.gardeningknowhow.com/ornamental/flowers/roses/
harvesting-rose-seeds.htm

33 Schein, E. (1987). *Process Consultation: Lessons for Managers and
Consultants.* Cambridge, MA: Addison-Wesley. p 94-114

34 www.patagonia.com

[35] Lewin, K. (1951). *Field Theory in Social Science: selected theoretical papers (Edited by Dorwin Cartwright.).* Harpers.

[36] Von Bertalanffy, L. (1968). *General Systems Theory: Foundations, Development, Application.* New York: George Braziller, Inc.

[37] https://systemsandus.com/foundations/why-you-should-think-like-a-modeler/balancing-loops/

[38] https://www.isc.hbs.edu/about-michael-porter/biography/Pages/default.aspx

[39] https://boxaroundtheworld.com/mcdonalds-supply-chain-management/

[40] https://www.freep.com/story/money/cars/2021/06/15/car-chip-shortage-2021/7688773002/#:~:text=What%20is%20the%20chip%20shortage%3F%20The%20chip%20shortage,of%20thousands%20of%20vehicles%20parked%20awaiting%20chip%20parts

[41] https://www.techrepublic.com/article/global-chip-shortage-the-logjam-is-holding-up-more-than-laptops-and-cars-and-could-spoil-the-holidays

[42] https://www.cnbc.com/2021/05/14/chip-shortage-expected-to-cost-auto-industry-110-billion-in-2021.html#:~:text=The%20semiconductor%20chip%20shortage%20is%20expected%20to%20cost,initial%20forecast%20of%20%2460.6%20billion%20in%20late%20January.

[43] https://www.wcpo.com/money/consumer/dont-waste-your-money/paper-and-lumber-prices-soaring-in-2021

[44] https://www.forbes.com/sites/forbestechcouncil/2019/02/05/10-industries-on-the-cusp-of-technological-disruption/?sh=5c12a3e55d47

[45] Martin, K. (1959). *A Cap For Kathy.* New York: Golden Press

[46] https://web.archive.org/web/20101119080037/http://medicine.yale.edu/emergencymed/whatis.aspx

[47] https://www.irs.gov/taxtopics/tc762

[48] https://www.reuters.com/article/us-uber-lawsuit/u-s-judge-says-uber-drivers-are-not-companys-employees.

49 https://scholar.google.com/scholar_case

50 https://www.employerslawyersblog.com/2018/07/california-supreme-court-changes-test-for-independent-contractor-status.html.

51 https://sacramento.cbslocal.com/2020/10/08/uber-lyft-california-contractors-prop-22/

52 https://www.law360.com/employment-authority/articles/1344185/uber-lyft-drivers-ask-calif-justices-to-invalidate-prop-22

53 Wohlleben, Peter. (2016). *The Hidden Life of Trees, What They Feel, How They Communicate.* Berkely, CA: Greystone Books, Ltd.

54 https://www.nps.gov/parkhistory/online_books/shirley/sec11.htm

55 https://www.goodreads.com/author/quotes/1113469.Hermann_Hesse

56 https://www.businessnewsdaily.com/8122-oldest-companies-in-america.html

57 Deming, W.E. (1982). *Out of the Crisis.* Cambridge, MA: MIT Center for Advanced Engineering Study

58 https://money.cnn.com/magazines/fortune/fortune_archive/1988/02/01/70146/index.htm#:~:text=Now%20that%20the%20breakup%20has%20finally%20taken%20place%2C,Sony%20secured%20the%20rights%20in%20the%201950s%20

59 https://www.computerhistory.org/siliconengine/bell-labs-licenses-transistor-technology/

60 The very public failures of 16 famous businesses: https://www.lovemoney.com/gallerylist/65252/the-very-public-failures-of-16-famous-businesses

61 https://qz.com/1660465/the-way-spotify-and-apple-music-pays-artists-isnt-fair/#:~:text=The%20way%20Spotify%20and%20Apple%20Music%20pay%20artists,the%20total%20share%20of%20streams%20each%20artist%20received.

62 Von Bertalanffy, Ludwig. (1968). *General Systems Theory: Foundations, Development, Applications.* New York, NY: George Braziller, Inc.

63 *ibid*

[64] https://nature.berkeley.edu/garb

[65] https://jamesclear.com/entropy

[66] https://marinedebris.noaa.gov/info/patch.html

[67] https://www.nationalgeographic.org/encyclopedia/great-pacific-garbage-patch/

[68] https://www.thecentersquare.com/california/more-people-died-from-drug-overdoses-in-san-francisco-this-year-than-from-coronavirus/article_8bcdaca0-4865-11eb-99a5-ef08390c1ec8.html

[69] https://theurbandeveloper.com/articles/ocean-cleanup-tackles-great-pacific-garbage-patch-akte-two

[70] https://kprcradio.iheart.com/featured/the-pursuit-of-happiness/content/2019-04-26-california-ban-straws-but-passes-out-thousands-of-free-syringes-to-junkies/

[71] https://www.worldwildlife.org/stories/forest-fires-the-good-and-the-bad

[72] Francesco, M. et al (2009). *Forensic Science International.* PMID: 19467810 DOI: 10.1016/j.forsciint.2009.04.018

[73] https://www.independent.co.uk/news/uk/home-news/cocaine-use-britain-so-high-it-has-contaminated-our-drinking-water-report-shows-9350477.html

[74] https://www.theguardian.com/environment/2018/jun/21/cocaine-in-rivers-harming-endangered-eels-study-finds

[75] https://www.nationalgeographic.com/news/2018/06/european-eels-on-cocaine-polluted-rivers-science-environment-animals/

[76] O'Boyle, T., *WSJ*, May 7, 1990; Chegg.com

[77] LeDuff, C. (2013). *Detroit: An American Autopsy.* New York, NY: Penguin Press

[78] Highsmith, J. (2004). *Agile Project Management.* Boston, MA: Pearson Education, Inc.

[79] Larson, Erik W., Gray, Clifford F. (2011). *Project Management the Managerial Process,* 5th ed. New York: McGraw Hill

80 http://www.Code.org

81 Holland, J. H. (1992/1975). *Adaptation in Natural and Artificial Systems: An Introductory Analysis with Applications to Biology, Control, and Artificial Intelligence.* Boston, MA: MIT Press

82 Porter-O'Grady, T., Malloch, K. (2007). *Quantum Leadership: A Resource for Health Care Innovation.* Sudbury, MA: Jones and Bartlett Publishers

83 https://www.britannica.com/science/chaos-theory

84 https://www.ncbi.nlm.nih.gov/pmc/articles/PMC3202497/

85 Porter-O'Grady, T., Malloch, K. (2007). *Quantum Leadership: A Resource for Health Care Innovation.* Sudbury, MA: Jones and Bartlett Publishers. p 31

86 Shafritz, Jay M., Ott, Steven J. (2001). *Classics of Organizational Theory,* 5th ed. Fort Worth: Harcourt College Publishers

87 Fayol, Henri. (1949). *General and Industrial Management.* Trans. Constance Storrs. London: Pittman Publishing. p 19-42 (original work published 1916)

88 Shafritz, J.M., Ott, M., *Classics in Organization Theory,* 5th ed., Fort Worth: Harcourt College Publishers, p 152-157 (source: Henry Metcalf, ed, *Scientific Foundations of Business Administration,* Baltimore: Williams and Wilkins, 1926)

89 Shafritz, J.M., Ott, J.S., Suk Jang, S. (2011). *Classics of Organization Theory,* 7th ed. Boston, MA: Wadsworth Cengage Learning; Minzberg, H. "The Five Parts of the Organization." p 222-233, adapted from *The Structure of the Organization: A Synthesis of the of.* p 18-34. Upper Saddle River, NJ: Pearson Education, Inc.

90 Johnson, D.W., Johnson, F.P., (2006). *Joining Together: Group Theory and Group Skills,* 9th ed. Boston, MA: Pearson (original Hersey P., Blanchard K., *Management of Organizational Behavior: Utilizing Human Resources,* 3rd ed. Englewood Cliffs, NJ: Prentice-Hall

91 Bennis, Warren. (1989). *On Becoming a Leader.* Reading, MA: Addison-Wesley

92 Schein, E.H. (1992). *Organizational Culture and Leadership,* 2nd ed., San Francisco, CA: Jossey-Bass

[93] Moss-Kanter, R. (1983). *The Change Masters: Innovation for Productivity in the American Corporation.* New York, NY: Simon and Shuster.

[94] Senge, P. (1990). *The Fifth Discipline: The Art and Practice of The Learning Organization.* New York: Doubleday/Currency

[95] https://hbr.org/1979/03/how-competitive-forces-shape-strategy

[96] https://www.isc.hbs.edu/about-michael-porter/biography/Pages/default.aspx

[97] Shafritz, J.M., Ott, M., *Classics in Organization Theory*, 5th ed., Fort Worth, TX: Harcourt College Publishers, "General Principles of Management" by Fayol, H. p 48-60

[98] Shafritz, J.M., Ott, M., *Classics in Organization Theory*, 5th ed., Fort Worth, TX: Harcourt College Publishers, "The Bases of Social Power" by French, J.R.P., Raven, B., p 319-328

[99] DePree, Max. (1992). *Leadership Jazz.* New York: Dell Publishing. P 119

[100] DePree, Max. (2004). *Leadership is an Art.* New York: Doubleday

[101] *ibid*, p 120

[102] *ibid*, p 184

[103] Peters, Tom, Waterman, Robert H. Jr., (1982), *In Search of Excellence.* Broadway, New York: Harper-Collins

[104] http://mastersinvest.com/newblog/2019/7/5/learning-from-costcos-jim-sinegal

[105] https://www.thestrategywatch.com/leadership-qualities-style-traits-skills-james-sinegal/#:~:text=He%20leads%20from%20the%20floor.%20James%20Sinegal%20never,Costco's%20warehouses%-20at%20least%20200%20times%20a%20year.

[106] https://www.nist.gov/baldrige

[107] https://www.pacifichorticulture.org/articles/ralph-moore-father-of-the-miniature-rose/

[108] https://davesgarden.com/guides/articles/view/1059

109 https://www.pacifichorticulture.org/articles/ralph-moore-father-of-the-miniature-rose/

110 https://www.davidaustinroses.com/pages/david-c-h-austin

111 http://www.lakesideorganic.com/media-room/organic-king-dick-peixoto-grows-and-gives-big/

112 https://ofrf.org/news/a-visit-to-lakeside-organic-gardens/

113 Iaccoca, L. (2007). *Where Have All The Leaders Gone?*. New York, NY: Scribner

114 *Leading in a Time of Change: What It Will Take To Lead in the Future.* A conversation with Peter F. Drucker and Peter M. Senge. (2001). Video: Drucker Foundation.

115 https://www.ibm.com/ibm/history/ibm100/us/en/icons/think_culture/team

116 https://computerhistory.org/blog/the-hp-ways-lessons-on-strategy-and-culture/?key=the-hp-ways-lessons-on-strategy-and-culture

117 Walton, Sam, Huey. (1992). *Made in America.* New York, NY: Doubleday Press

118 https://www.cbsnews.com/news/the-mensch-of-malden-mills/

119 CBS "60 Minutes" *The Mensch of Malden Mill* that aired July 3, 2003

120 https://www.marriott.com/about/culture-and-values/history.mi

121 https://www.icmrindia.org/CaseStudies/catalogue/Business%20Ethics/The%20Johnson%20&%20Johnson%20Tylenol%20Controversies.htm

122 https://www.marriott.com/about/culture-and-values/history.mi

123 Roddick, Anita. (1991). *Body and Soul: Profits with Principles.* Britain, UK: Ebury Press

124 Chouinard, Yvon. (2005). *Let My People Go Surfing: The Education of a Reluctant Businessman.* London: Penquin Group

125 https://www.forbes.com/sites/willyakowicz/2020/03/16/at-billionaire-owned-patagonia-outdoor-clothing-chain-employees-to-be-paid-despite-store-closures-amid-coronavirus/?sh=2c1aeb2e7edd

[126] *Paul Orfalea on Creating the Kinko's Brand, Forbes.com:* https://www.forbes.com/sites/danschawbel/2012/06/28/paul-orfalea-on-creating-the-kinkos-brand/#e6280bc3f01

[127] Orfalea, P. (2009). *Two Billion Dollars in Nickels-Reflections on the Entrepreneurial Life.* Charleston, NC: BookSurge Publishing

[128] G. James Lemoine, Chad A. Hartnell, and Hannes Leroy, 2019: *Taking Stock of Moral Approaches to Leadership: An Integrative Review of Ethical, Authentic, and Servant Leadership.* annuls, **13**, 148–187, https://doi.org/10.5465/annals.2016.0121

[129] https://www.greenleaf.org/what-is-servant-leadership/

[130] https://www.forbes.com/sites/robdube/2019/11/25/this-ceo-of-a-billion-dollar-tech-company-built-a-retreat-center-where-leaders-can-unplug-grow-and-look-within/?sh=3a0ee587734d

[131] Schein, Edgar H. (1992). *Organizational Culture and Leadership,* 2nd ed. San Francisco: Jossey-Bass

[132] *ibid* p 12

[133] https://computerhistory.org/blog/the-hp-ways-lessons-on-strategy-and-culture/?key=the-hp-ways-lessons-on-strategy-and-culture

[134] https://www.statista.com/topics/4891/gig-economy-in-the-us/

[135] http://http-download.intuit.com/http.intuit/CMO/intuit/futureofsmallbusiness/intuit_2020_report.pdf

[136] https://history.library.ucsf.edu/stanford_merger.html

[137] *ibid*

[138] *ibid*

[139] https://news.stanford.edu/news/1999/august11/restructure-811.html

[140] https://www.healthaffairs.org/doi/pdf/10.1377/hlthaff.18.2.143

[141] https://stanfordmag.org/contents/the-anatomy-of-a-failed-hospital-merger

[142] https://history.library.ucsf.edu/stanford_merger.html.

[143] https://stanfordmag.org/contents/the-anatomy-of-a-failed-hospital-merger

[144] https://news.stanford.edu/news/1999/august11/resign-811.html

[145] https://www.sfgate.com/health/article/End-of-an-ER-Mount-Zion-s-emergency-room-closes-2892669.php#photo-2242997

[146] https://williamwolff.org/wp-content/uploads/2016/01/griffin-groupthink-challenger.pdf

[147] https://boingboing.net/2019/12/03/collective-rationalization.html

[148] Gawande, Atul. (2009). *The Checklist Manifesto: How to Get Things Right.* New York: Metropolitan Books

[149] Nicholas, John M. (2001). *Project Management for Business and Technology: Principles and Practice,* 2nd ed. Upper Saddle River, NJ: Prentice Hall.

[150] https://www.nasa.gov/pdf/49652main_okeefe_caib_transcript.pdf

[151] Argyris, Chris (1990). *Overcoming Organizational Defenses: Facilitating Organizational Learning.* Needham Heights: Allen and Bacon

[152] Drucker, Peter. (1963). "Managing for Business Effectiveness." Harvard Business Review.

[153] https://deming.org/deming/deming-the-man

[154] Sandberg, Sheryl. (2013). *Lean In: Women, Work and the Will to Lead.* New York: Knopf, Borzoi Books. p 148

[155] https://www.cbsnews.com/news/making-a-team-greater-than-the-sum-of-its-parts/

[156] Larson, Erik W., Gray, Clifford F. (2011). *Project Management: The Managerial Process,* 5th ed. New York: McGraw Hill

[157] Senge, Peter. (1990). *The Fifth Discipline: The Art and Practice of the Learning Organization.* New York: Doubleday.

[158] Tuckman, Bruce. *Psychological Bulletin,* 1965, Vol. 63, No.6, p 384-396

[159] George, Jennifer M., Jones, Gareth R. (2002). *Organizational Behavior,* 3rd ed. Upper Saddle River, NJ: Prentice Hall, p 373

[160] Schwarz, Roger. (2002). *The Skilled Facilitator.* San Francisco: Jossey-Bass. p 19

[161] Walker, Arthur H., Lorsch, Jay W. (1968). *Organizational Choice: Product versus Function. Harvard Business Review.* Reprinted in *Classics of Organizational Theory,* 5th ed. (2001). Edited by Shafritz, Jay M., Ott, Steven J. Fort Worth: Harcourt Brace p 211 2

[162] http://web.mit.edu/curhan/www/docs/Articles/15341_Readings/Group_Performance/Sundstrom_et_al_1990_Work_Teams.pdf

[163] Welch, Jack. Welch, Suzy. (2005). *Winning.* NY: Harper Collins

[164] Argyris, Chris. (1990). *Overcoming Organizational Defenses: Facilitating Organizational Learning.* NY: Wiley&Sons

[165] *Ibid*

[166] *Ibid*

[167] George, Jennifer M., Jones, Gareth R. (2002). *Organizational Behavior 3rd ed..* New Jersey: Prentice Hall.

[168] *Ibid*

[169] Argyris, Chris. (1993). *Knowledge for Action: A Guide to Overcoming Barriers to Organizational Change,* 1st ed. San Francisco: Jossey-Bass

[170] *Ibid*

[171] Malsbury, Erin. "Paws and Effects." *Good Times,* "Paws and Effects" July 7-13.

[172] https://www.mbari.org/pandemic-reduced-ocean-noise/

[173] http://www.santacruzpumas.org

[174] https://www.theguardian.com/environment/2020/sep/13/killer-whales-launch-orchestrated-attacks-on-sailing-boats

[175] https://www.mercurynews.com/2020/05/10/santa-cruz-surfer-killed-in-shark-attack-identified/

[176] https://www.washingtonpost.com/local/public-safety/gun-and-ammunition-sales-rise-amid-pandemic-fears/2020/03/21/6000640e-6b08-11ea-abef-020f086a3fab_story.html

[177] https://www.ctpost.com/news/article/California-fires-claim-5-lives-threaten-15503678.php

[178] https://www.nytimes.com/2020/08/11/us/homicides-crime-kansas-city-coronavirus.html

179 https://www.washingtonpost.com/local/public-safety/gun-and-ammunition-sales-rise-amid-pandemic-fears/2020/03/21/6000640e-6b08-11ea-abef-020f086a3fab_story.html

180 https://nymag.com/intelligencer/2021/02/america-saw-a-historic-rise-in-murders-in-2020-why.html

181 https://www.bbc.com/news/world-us-canada-53224445

182 https://www.city-journal.org/antifa-seattle-capitol-hill-autonomous-zone

183 https://bayareagazette.com/san-francisco-overdose-deaths-far-exceeded-2020-covid-19-deaths-nationally/#:~:text=%28The%20Center%20Square%29%20%E2%80%93%20Almost%20three%20times%20as,compared%20with%20255%20who%20died%20from%20the%20coronavirus.

184 https://pubmed.ncbi.nlm.nih.gov/32539153/

185 https://www.cdc.gov/mmwr/volumes/69/wr/mm6932a1.htm

186 https://fortune.com/2021/04/01/restaurants-closed-2020-pandemic-100000-jobs-lost-how-many-have-closed-us-covid-pandemic-stimulus-unemployment/

187 https://www.weforum.org/agenda/2021/05/america-united-states-covid-small-businesses-economics/

188 https://www.cdc.gov/mmwr/volumes/69/wr/mm6943a3.html

189 https://fortune.com/2021/10/18/amazon-massive-growth-covid-pandemic-8-charts

190 Barrero, Jose Maria, et al. (April, 2021). *Why Working From Home Will Stick*. Ronzetti Initiative for the Study of Labor Markets , Becker Friedman Institute.

191 https://www.weforum.org/agenda/2021/11/what-is-the-great-resignation-and-what-can-we-learn-from-it/

192 Senge, Peter. (1990). *The Fifth Discipline: The Art and Practice of the Learning Organization.* New York: Doubleday Currency, p.1

193 Cummings, Thomas G., Worley, Christopher G., (2005). *Organization Development and Change,* 8th ed. Mason, Ohio: South-Western

About the Author

Kathleen is a businesswoman, researcher, professor, and mother. Kathleen became an emergency department nurse at 21 and by 28 embarked upon an entrepreneurial mission to change the model of nursing practice. She holds a Bachelor of Science in Nursing, Master of Business Administration, Master of Information Systems and Doctor of Education, Organization and Leadership. As a principal consultant in NakIV Health and professor, Doctor Nakfoor both applied and taught organizational theory for over twenty years. For thirty years she has honed her horticultural craft, crisscrossing a journey that has traversed both business and a passion for gardening.